Imagine You Walked with Jesus:
A Guide to Ignatian Contemplative Prayer

Imagine
You Walked
with
Jesus

A GUIDE TO

Ignatian Contemplative Prayer

JERRY WINDLEY-DAOUST

Our Sunday Visitor
Huntington, Indiana

Nihil Obstat
Msgr. Michael Heintz, Ph.D.
Censor Librorum

Imprimatur
✠ Kevin C. Rhoades
Bishop of Fort Wayne-South Bend
August 23, 2021

The *Nihil Obstat* and *Imprimatur* are official declarations that a book is free from doctrinal or moral error. It is not implied that those who have granted the *Nihil Obstat* and *Imprimatur* agree with the contents, opinions, or statements expressed.

Our Sunday Visitor Publishing Division
Our Sunday Visitor, Inc.
200 Noll Plaza
Huntington, IN 46750
www.osv.com
1-800-348-2440

ISBN: 978-1-68192-703-9 (Inventory No. T2581)
RELIGION—Christian Living—Prayer.
RELIGION—Biblical Meditations—New Testament.
RELIGION—Christianity—Catholic.
eISBN: 978-1-68192-704-6
LCCN: 2021949931

Cover and interior design: Lindsey Riesen
Cover art: Adobe Stock

PRINTED IN THE UNITED STATES OF AMERICA

For my wife, Susan, whose spiritual companionship has been so important to my own walk with Jesus

Contents

Imaginative Prayer:
A Way to Walk with Jesus

Imagine, for a moment, that some technological genius has invented a time machine, and you are selected to take it for a test ride. You can go to any time and place in the past, on the condition that you meet a famous historical figure and return to tell the modern world all about him or her.

As a Christian, you wonder what it would be like to meet Jesus, face to face ... to walk with him along the roads, fields, and seashores of ancient Palestine. You could see his miracles and hear his parables. You might even approach him ... talk to him, ask him questions, seek his healing touch.

What would that be like? Would you jump at the chance, full of excitement and enthusiasm ... or would you hesitate, a little intimidated? This *is* the Son of God, after all!

Maybe you would be afraid of being disappointed. Perhaps you would decide to keep your distance, mingling in the crowds that follow him. Or maybe you would approach some of his close followers first — Peter or Martha, for example — in the hope that they might introduce you.

Time machines do not exist, of course. But there is another way to "meet" Jesus that is actually *better* than a time machine. This way is not powered by plutonium or Artron energy, but by your imagination and the Holy Spirit; appropriately enough, it is called *imaginative prayer*.

Saint Ignatius and the Power of the Imagination

People have used their imaginations in prayer since forever, but the method of imaginative prayer I am inviting you to experience in this book was popularized nearly five hundred years ago by a Spanish nobleman named Iñigo Lopez de Oñaz y Loyola, better known today as St. Ignatius of Loyola.

From his youth, Iñigo was a dreamer. Fueled by popular books of adventure and romance, he imagined the glory he would win for himself with heroic deeds. Those dreams led him to a soldier's life, and eventually, to a fateful battle. In the spring of 1521, a French army attacked the fortress town of Pamplona. His comrades proposed surrendering (they were outnumbered fourteen to one), but Iñigo persuaded them to fight on. During the battle, a French cannonball shattered his leg.

He was taken back to the Loyola family castle, where he spent nine months recovering. Bored, he asked for books to read — preferably ones about romance and adventure. Instead, he was given two popular religious books: *The Golden Legend* by Jacobus de Varagine (a medieval collection of stories about the saints) and *The Life of Christ* by Ludolph of Saxony.

Iñigo at once began bringing what he read to life in his imagination. He spent long hours daydreaming about the great deeds he could do in service to Christ, just like the saints in *The Golden Legend*. And with the encouragement of *The Life of Christ*, he vividly imagined various scenes from the Gospels, too. He took notes as he read, eventually filling a three-hundred-page notebook.

These daydreams alternated with his typical fantasies about the great things he might do in the royal court or on the battlefield. Gradually, he noticed something about these different experiences. His dreams of winning personal glory left him feeling empty and restless, but his dreams of winning glory for God made him peaceful and content. Gradually, he realized that different spiritual forces lay behind these feelings.

Here, at the beginning of his new life, Iñigo had discovered a truth that would form the basis of his spirituality: All created things, including human emotions and imagination, have the potential to make us holy — that is, to bring us into a richer, more intimate relationship with God.

Years later, Ignatius and six companions joined together to form a new religious order, the Society of Jesus (popularly known as the Jesuits). Ignatius wrote a sort of "spiritual training manual" for the Jesuits based on notes he had kept during his recovery and the years of prayer and study that followed. He called this manual the *Spiritual Exercises*. Not surprisingly, imaginative prayer was a key element of the exercises.

The Practice of Imaginative Prayer

Let's look at the actual practice of imaginative prayer — or, as Jesuits call it, contemplative prayer. (This term has a completely different meaning in the rest of the Christian prayer tradition, so we will keep using the term *imaginative prayer* here.)

Saint Ignatius believed that God intended for the human imagination to draw us closer to him. He was well aware that the imagination can just as easily separate us from God, of course. But imaginative prayer is different from idle or directionless daydreaming in two key ways:

1. It is powered not just by our imagination, but by the Holy Spirit working through our imagination.
2. It is rooted in a sacred text, usually the Gospels.

In imaginative prayer, the same Holy Spirit who inspired the authors of the Gospels also *inspires* (literally "breathes into") our imaginations in a way that draws us closer to Christ. Prayer is a conversation with God; imaginative prayer creates a space for that encounter.

The heart of imaginative prayer, then, is to "meet" God, usually in the person of Jesus, in a *personal* way.

Often when we read or hear a Scripture passage, we do so from a safe distance, just skimming its surface or analyzing it intellectually. Imaginative prayer does not let us off the hook so easily: We stand right alongside Jesus as he navigates the challenges of everyday life — hunger, death, sickness, conflict, exclusion — in a specific time and place. Whether he is calling out the Pharisees for their religious hypocrisy, healing a sick woman, offering the incredulous crowds living bread, or rescuing Peter from drowning, Jesus catches our eye, asking: *And what about you?*

With all this in mind, let's go over the basic method of imaginative prayer. At the same time, we will look at how *Imagine You Walked with Jesus* guides and encourages your imaginative prayer experience.

1. Choose a Scripture passage

First, choose a suitable Scripture text. Although imaginative prayer can be used with any sacred text (including stories from the lives of the saints), Saint Ignatius recommended contemplating scenes from the Gospels; they are the primary texts in which we encounter the Son of God "in the flesh."

The ideal text will be a story about Jesus, rather than one of his discourses or parables. Yes, you could meditate on the Sermon on the Mount (Mt 5–7), imagining yourself among the crowds listening to Jesus. However, your focus would likely be on the content and meaning of Jesus' words. This is not a bad thing; it is just different from the type of prayer that we are pursuing here.

In this book: The main part of this book includes the text of forty Gospel stories that are good for imaginative prayer. Each story is briefly introduced under the "Walk with Jesus" heading.

If you pray your way through the forty stories in this book from beginning to end, you will follow a rough outline of the events of Jesus' life. Alternatively, you can jump around the book, or try one of the reading plans beginning on page 225.

2. Prepare with prayer

Rather than diving right into the Scripture or other sacred reading, Saint Ignatius suggests we first prepare ourselves. Find a quiet and comfortable place to pray and take a few moments to settle in: Close the door, turn off distracting electronics, and get comfortable. Then take a few moments to pray along these lines:

1. Begin by becoming aware that God is already here waiting for you. Rest in his loving presence.
2. Then respond to God's loving presence by giving yourself over to him. Pray that you might love and serve him in all your thoughts, words, and actions.

Prayer is fundamentally an expression of our relationship with God. When we begin by acknowledging God's availability to us and by making ourselves available to God in return, we situate everything that happens next within that relationship. This is not a project we undertake on our own, for our own benefit; rather, this is a journey we are making *with* God and *for* God.

You can think of this moment as analogous to the greeting that two friends exchange when they first meet one another; it does not need to last long before you move into the heart of your time of prayer.

In this book: In each reading, the "Prepare" heading will guide you through this preparatory prayer. Make the movements of this prayer your own as the Holy Spirit prompts you.

3. Read the Scripture

Next, read the Scripture passage at least once.

You may wish to ask the Holy Spirit to help you to read the text prayerfully. Given the amount of reading most of us do online, you may be in the habit of skimming the text rather than ruminating on the words. Try to slow down; the Gospels were written slowly and intentionally. Each word and phrase, and each omission, was chosen for a reason. Stay with the words and see what they serve up.

In this book: This book provides the text of each story from the *New Revised Standard Version, Catholic Edition.*

If you revisit a favorite Gospel story several times, you may want to explore other translations as well; other suggested translations of the Bible are included in the "Walk with Jesus Again" section beginning on page 203.

4. Set the scene

After you have read the story at least once, use your imagination to set the scene. Be as specific about the details as possible, engaging all your senses: touch, smell, sound, sight … even taste, if the opportunity arises. Make the Gospel story come vividly to life, almost as if you were directing a movie. The Son of God chose to save us not merely with a word from heaven, but by becoming the Word-made-flesh at a specific time and place in human history. In imagining the Gospel in its physical setting, we honor the reality of Jesus' Incarnation, and set the stage for encountering him "in the flesh" ourselves.

One of the most important details to consider is how you will enter the story: Who will you be? Where will you stand in relation to Jesus? The role you choose to play will dramatically affect how your prayer experience unfolds. Take, for example, the story of the woman caught in adultery (reading guide #22, page 121). Choosing to be the woman will lead to a much different prayer experience than choosing to be one of her accusers. And choosing to be an uninvolved observer (one of the disciples, for instance) will place you at a safe distance from the action. Someone might have good reason to keep their distance — the trauma of a sexual assault, for instance. But in general, you want to take up a position that involves you in the action of the story and brings you into contact with Jesus.

Here are some things to consider as you set the stage for your imaginative prayer experience:

- Who are you in this story?
- What time of day is it? What is the weather like?
- What do you see around you? If you are outdoors, what kinds of plants, crops, buildings, or animals do you see? If you are indoors, what does the space look like?
- Who is present? What do they look like, and what are they doing? What do their movements and facial expressions communicate about their thoughts and feelings?
- What ambient sounds do you hear? The distant murmur of a marketplace? Seagulls and crashing waves? Crying children, or bleating goats?
- How do you feel? Hot? Hungry? Tired?
- What do you smell? Olive oil? Perfume? Animal dung or cooking fires? Sweat? The salty breezes of the ocean?
- Above all, be sure to pay attention to Jesus. Where

does he stand? What does he do? What does his face
communicate? What about his movements, and tone
of voice?

In this book: This book presents historical, geographical, and
cultural background for each Gospel story. You will find this information in "A Brief Tour of First-Century Palestine" (page 21).
Each reading also includes background information specific to its
Gospel story under its "Set the Scene" section.

The purpose of this information is to place you on a more even
footing with the Gospels' first audience, the Christians of first-century Palestine. Many of these details — the layout of a typical
house, the dangers of boating on the Sea of Galilee — would have
been known to these first hearers of the Gospel, but are not so obvi-
ous to modern readers. These details may help you "fill in the gaps"
of the Gospel story, making for a richer imaginative experience.

The "Set the Scene" section concludes with a handful of
prompt questions; these are intended to be helpful reminders, not a
definitive or exhaustive checklist.

5. Walk with Jesus

Once you have "composed" the setting of the story, put aside the
text and let yourself enter into it. This is the body of your imaginative prayer, so take as much time here as you need.

Saint Ignatius suggests bookending your time with Jesus with
an opening prayer and a closing prayer.

Before stepping into the Gospel, Saint Ignatius advises that you
pray for what you most desire from this encounter with Jesus. This
might be something general: a meaningful encounter with Jesus,
for example, or a strengthening of virtue. Or it might be something
more specific, like healing from a traumatic experience, insight
into a difficult problem, or the gift of peace during a turbulent time.

Next, enter the Gospel, letting the action of the story unfold by itself under the direction of the Holy Spirit; do not actively direct or force the actions of the main characters. Your role is to participate in the action of the story in whatever way seems natural. You might offer to help Martha at the cooking fire, for example, or you might lead the colt for Jesus as he rides into Jerusalem. You might find yourself replying to other characters' questions or engaging in conversation with them. You might even find yourself interacting directly with Jesus.

Do not be surprised if it feels challenging to let the Spirit lead your prayer; many of us feel more comfortable being in control of our own agenda. We may resist being led into unfamiliar territory or having our fundamental assumptions challenged or upended (even by Jesus!). If that describes you, take that part of yourself to the Holy Spirit, too. Then relax, and tap into the same curiosity, spontaneity, and openness that (hopefully) fueled your play as a child.

A word of caution: During imaginative prayer, we are not primarily concerned with achieving historical accuracy; if the Holy Spirit leads you to imagine that Peter's fishing boat bears a strong resemblance to your grandfather's old Lund outboard, by all means, follow the promptings of the Spirit!

Finally, as you step out of the Gospel story, speak to God directly. Saint Ignatius refers to this as a "colloquy," or a spiritual conversation. He invites us to share our thoughts, feelings, and desires with God, much as one friend would speak to another.

Ideally, this will flow naturally from your immersion in the Gospel story. For example, after contemplating Peter's miraculous catch of fish from the perspective of Peter, you might realize that your financial worries have led you to "fishing all night without catching anything." As you finish imagining the Gospel story, you might begin speaking to God directly about your financial worries. You might share your frustration and ask for the grace to trust God more. You might even ask for a miraculous catch of fish!

To get a feel for what this "spiritual conversation with God" might look like, check out the five examples of imaginative prayer, each written by a different person, in the back of this book (pages 207–214). Nelly Sosa, for instance, moves quickly from walking with the risen Jesus to pouring out her heart to him in prayer: "Please listen to the prayers in my heart ... hear my sadness, my confusion, my frustration. But above all ... let me hear you ... let me see your face ..." (you can read her reflection on page 213). In another example, Rachelle Linner doesn't hesitate to bring feelings of anger, gratitude, and joy to prayer as she reflects on the Gospel story of Jesus' healing of a blind man (you can read her reflection on page 219).

Saint Ignatius advises us that the emotions we experience during our encounter with Jesus are signposts that reveal something about our spiritual life. Some of those emotions might be pleasant (joy, gratitude, peace, wonder), though others may not be (anger, fear, sadness, guilt, confusion). Whatever emotions surface during your imaginative prayer, bring them to Jesus now ... and in the hours and days that follow. Ask the Holy Spirit to reveal God's grace and invitation in these feelings.

Saint Ignatius recommends that we close our time of prayer with the Lord's Prayer; you might substitute another formal prayer that you like, such as the Glory Be or a simple Sign of the Cross. The point is to punctuate the end of this special time with Jesus.

In this book: The "Walk with Jesus" section guides you through the three moments in this part of your prayer: first, praying for what your heart desires; next, letting the Holy Spirit be your guide as you enter the Gospel story; and finally, pouring out your heart in a conversation with God.

6. Reflect on the journey

After you are finished praying, spend some time reflecting on your encounter with Jesus. You can do this immediately after your prayer, or as you go about the rest of your day. If you are using this book on your own, you might record your reflection in a journal or notebook. If you are using this book with a prayer group, set aside some time to share and discuss your prayer experience.

This period of reflection may flow naturally from a good prayer experience. In other cases, you may need to be more intentional about it. Either way, this time of reflection will greatly aid your growth in prayer and help you more fully realize and accept the gift you have just received.

In this book: The "Reflect on the Journey" section includes several optional reflection questions; these may be useful for individual reflection or small-group discussion.

• • •

Some people wonder: How do I know that my prayer experience comes from the Holy Spirit, and not something of my own making? Prayer is always a dialogue, of course, so you are responsible for part of the experience. However, Saint Ignatius would encourage you to ask: "Did this prayer experience lead me closer to God, or farther away?" The answer to that question is a good measure of whether the Holy Spirit — or some other spirit — was at work in you.

Journaling Your Prayer Experience

If you like writing, you may find it particularly fruitful to write about the Gospel story as you experienced it during your prayer. You can record your experience in a bound journal, notebook, blog, or any other format that works for you.

If you choose to journal your prayer experience, you will probably want to spend some time freely imagining the story before you begin writing. If you begin writing immediately after reading the Gospel story, your writing brain may "speak over" your imagination (and the promptings of the Holy Spirit). Do not worry about the quality of your writing — not the punctuation, not the grammar, not the "flow" of the words. People more inclined to creative writing may enjoy writing in a more narrative style, but if that's not you, let go of that expectation. Instead, simply make short notes of your impressions and feelings. You can find five examples of journal entries based on imaginative prayer beginning on page 207.

If you are lucky enough to have a spiritual director, you might like to share your journal entries with that person as part of your spiritual direction. Even if you never share your journal entries with another person, save your writing so that you can read it again in the coming years. Saint Ignatius treasured his own spiritual journal for the rest of his life and no doubt returned to it often.

A Brief Tour of First-Century Palestine

Imaginative prayer is an intimate encounter with Jesus, not an archaeological expedition, so we are not overly concerned with historical accuracy. Still, knowing a little bit about the setting of the Gospels — the land, the people, and their culture — can help "fill in" details of the story that the Gospel's first-century audience would have known. These details can help us prayerfully enter the Gospel with the help of our imagination.

Each reading in this book includes background information particular to that entry's Gospel story. The following "tour" of first-century Palestine is meant to supplement those notes with more general background information.

If you would rather dive right in, go ahead and begin exploring the Gospel stories. When information from this "tour" might be helpful, you will find a note referring you back here.

• • •

For fun, let's return to the time-travel metaphor from the beginning of this book, imagining we are traveling back to first-century Palestine for a quick sightseeing tour.

Are you ready? Then get into your favorite time machine, and let's go!

What to Wear

Before you step out of your time machine, you are going to want to change clothes so that you can blend in.

First, put on a simple tunic. Made of soft wool or linen, this long, sleeveless garment falls below your knees and serves as your undergarment.

Now slip on an outer tunic — because going out with only the one tunic would be like going out in your underwear or nightgown back home. This one is made of finer cloth and more carefully sewn. Women's tunics are supposed to cover their ankles, while men's tunics may be somewhat shorter. You may see male slaves, soldiers, and other workers wearing shorter, knee-length tunics to allow for greater freedom of movement.

Now you will want a simple leather belt to keep your tunic from getting in your way as you work. Tie a leather bag or purse to the belt for carrying money, food, and other small items.

If you plan to visit the Temple or a synagogue, you'd better take along a veil or head covering. (It is also handy for protecting your head from the sun.) A leather circlet will hold it in place.

If the weather seems cool or rainy, bring along a heavy cloak. Take good care of it! It is probably your most expensive piece of clothing, and it doubles as your blanket on cool nights. You should always take your cloak with you when traveling overnight.

Unless you are very well off, you will need to make your own clothes from scratch, starting with the raw materials. Spinning, weaving, and sewing are skills that every Jewish girl learns from a young age. Your clothing will probably be the natural color of the wool or linen used to make it. Dye is expensive!

Finally, don't forget your footwear! You do *not* want to step out into the street without a sturdy pair of sandals. With wooden soles and leather straps, they are not the most comfortable, but they are better than nothing — the streets are dusty and full of animal droppings. Also, going barefoot is considered almost as shameful as going out naked.

Getting Around

As you walk with Jesus, you will probably be traveling by foot, which is how all but the richest people got around. On good roads and under ideal conditions, you might make twenty miles in a day … but most of the roads are not that great. Unless you are traveling on one of the paved Roman highways, your "road" may be more of a broad footpath.

Be sure to travel in a caravan or a large group; wild animals and bandits are a real threat for the lone traveler.

Although you might receive hospitality along the way, be prepared to provide your own food and water. Typical traveling fare will be bread, bread, and more bread … and if you are lucky, some herbs and olive oil to go with it.

Places to Go, People to See

Most of the action in the Gospels takes place in the geographical region known as Palestine; at the time of Jesus, this area was divided into three different kingdoms (all under Roman control): Galilee, in the north; Judea, in the south; and Samaria, which lay between the two.

Even though this area is relatively small — about 150 miles north to south, and between 30 and 50 miles wide from the Mediterranean coast to the Jordan River — both the land and its people vary greatly.

You will meet not only many different types of Jews as you

walk with Jesus, but also many types of non-Jews (Gentiles): Romans, Greeks, Persians, Syrians, Egyptians, and more. The Palestine that Jesus knew stood at the crossroads of many different cultures, with two great civilizations — those of the Greeks and the Romans — permeating them all.

Welcome to Galilee: Home of fishermen, farmers ... and a few rebels

Jesus grew up in Galilee, most of his apostles were from Galilee, and much of his ministry took place there, too. It is one of the most beautiful areas of the entire Middle East, with many streams, waterfalls, and green fields dotting the rocky, hilly terrain. It receives more rainfall than Judea, making it a fertile agricultural region. You will see fields of wheat and barley, as well as many groves of fruit trees — most importantly, olives, the oil of which was used for cooking, medicine, lamps, and religious rituals.

Galileans are fishermen and farmers known for their independent (and sometimes rebellious) spirit; they are sometimes regarded as "less Jewish" by Jews who live nearer to Jerusalem.

The area is heavily populated by non-Jews, with cities such as Tiberias and Sepphoris dominated by Greeks, Romans, and other foreigners. No wonder the Gospel of Matthew refers to it as "Galilee of the Gentiles"!

As you walk with Jesus in Galilee, you will spend time in these places:

- **Nazareth**, the home of Jesus' youth, is set on a hill about 1,200 feet above sea level, approximately twenty miles east of the Mediterranean Sea and fifteen miles southwest of the Sea of Galilee. It is a relatively small place, with perhaps fifty homes, a public bathhouse, and several springs. A high, rocky ridge lies to the south, but a broad, well-watered valley extends to the north, all the way to the more urbane administrative city of Sepphoris, about five miles away. No major roads pass through Nazareth; the village is truly off the beaten path.

- **Capernaum**, a fishing village of about one thousand people on the northern shore of the Sea of Galilee, is Jesus' "base of operations" during his ministry, and many stories from the Gospels are set there. Peter, Andrew, James, and John — all fishermen — lived in Capernaum, as did Matthew, the tax collector. Located at the crossroads of important trade routes, surrounded by fertile agricultural lands, and on the shore of one of the biggest fisheries in the area, Capernaum flourishes economically, as evidenced in its large, spacious buildings, many built from local basalt.
- The **Sea of Galilee** is a large freshwater lake about thirteen miles long and eight miles across; it is also sometimes called Lake Gennesaret or Lake Tiberias. It is a busy place, a thoroughfare for trade between the many Greek and Roman towns and settlements on its shores. It is also home to plentiful fisheries, and you will see dozens of fishing boats on its waters. Fish are salted and exported all over Palestine and the Roman Empire, giving the fishermen who ply its waters a very good living.

Now passing through Samaria

Samaria is the hilly region Jesus and his friends pass through whenever he travels from Galilee to Judea. Its principal city, Sebaste, was once the capital of the northern kingdom of Israel. King Herod I ("the Great") launched many building projects in the city, creating wide, colonnaded streets, temples, a stadium, and a theater. Samaritans claim that their version of Judaism is the true religion of the ancient Israelites. Samaritans worship in a temple they built on Mount Gerizim — which, according to their version of the Torah, is where God wanted the Temple built, not in Jerusalem. That claim does not sit well with the Jews of Galilee and Judea, who look down on Samaritans as not really Jewish at all.

Welcome to Judea

Judea is marked by hills and low mountains, the tallest of which is just over 3,300 feet high. The Jordan River marks its eastern boundary and drains into the Dead Sea, 1,312 feet below sea level. Farming gives way to herding as you move to the south and the east, with the land transitioning from scrubby wilderness to desert.

Jerusalem and the Temple

Jerusalem is located in the middle of the region and sits on a plateau in the Judean Mountains, about 2,500 feet above sea level. It is the largest city around, with perhaps one hundred thousand residents. Three times a year, during the festivals of Passover, Pentecost, and Booths, religious pilgrims flood the city, swelling the population to as many as a million people. During these festivals, the city is crowded not only with people, but with the animals they have brought to sacrifice at the Temple. The city is surrounded on all sides by tall, thick walls fortified with tall towers.

Jerusalem is divided into two main parts. The wealthy and the elite live in the neighborhoods of the Upper City, so called because it sprawls over a hill overlooking the rest of the city. King Herod I rebuilt much of the Upper City in the years before Jesus' birth, with blocks of large houses and mansions divided by wide streets, stately plazas, and public buildings. The city's wide main thoroughfares are paved with stones weighing as much as nineteen tons. An underground sewer system collects runoff water, and more than fifty miles of pipes and aqueducts supply water to the city's many ritual baths.

Although Jerusalem sits amid a range of low mountains,

the two most important are the Mount of Olives and the Temple Mount. The **Mount of Olives** is located just to the east of the city; it is named for the olive groves that cover its slopes, and it is also home to a huge, ancient cemetery dotted with thousands of hand-dug burial caves.

The **Temple Mount** is home to the magnificent Temple, expanded and refurbished by Herod the Great. The Temple is one of the largest and most splendid monuments in the world at this time; during festivals, it is an especially crowded, busy place.

The Temple sits on top of a hill that was extended by constructing retaining walls from enormous stone blocks as much as sixteen feet thick. These walls support a plaza measuring about 1,500 feet by 1,000 feet (about thirty-four acres), on which the Temple and its many buildings and courtyards were built.

Before entering the Temple, you will need to purify yourself in one of the ritual baths. Most pilgrims enter the Temple area via the southern entrance, with its huge gates and its grand staircase ascending three stories to the outer court (the "Court of the Gentiles"). Levites greet pilgrims at the entrance with music and songs. The Temple itself is a marvel of whitewashed stone and gold plating rising 150 feet above the plaza; the main entrance doors are made of bronze, and the roofline is topped in gold spikes to prevent birds from roosting there.

The outer court, surrounded by a colonnaded portico, is open to the public, including non-Jews; it is a busy bazaar, full of money changers, sacrificial animals, food and souvenir vendors, tour guides, teachers, and administrative buildings. Beyond the outer court is the Court of the Women, open to all Jews; beyond that lies the Court of the Israelites, open only to male Jews; and within that court is the Temple itself. Only priests can enter the Temple sanctuary.

Everyday Life: Family, Home, and Synagogue

During your journey with Jesus, plan to spend lots of time with ordinary people in their everyday lives. Here is some of what to expect.

Who is in charge around here?

The social structure of most societies in the ancient Near East, including Jewish society, can be summed up in this way: Family takes priority over individual freedom and choices.

The people of Jesus' time have a very generous definition of family that includes everyone living in a particular household, but also extends outward to include other blood relations. As the many genealogies in the Bible testify, the concept of family also extends back in time to include ancestors. Likewise, continuing the family line through one's descendants is of prime importance as well.

Communal, tribal, and national allegiance also trumps individual aspirations. One achieves honor by making a positive contribution to one's family, village, or nation — not by individual accomplishments.

Before you judge these people too harshly for their lack of individual freedoms, keep in mind that these ancient people live life on the edge. They do not have crop, health, or home insurance; they do not have Social Security or welfare; they cannot call on professional emergency responders with the push of three buttons; and they don't have labor unions or political representation. Mostly, all they have for a "safety net" is one another. That is why maintaining kin and communal relationships, along with a stable social order, is so important to them.

The social hierarchy of ancient Israel was well defined. Political and religious leaders hold the most honor and status, along with a small number of wealthy landowners and merchants. Skilled tradesmen are better off than tenant farmers and agricultural laborers, but even these are better off than those who are on the margins of society: slaves, people with chronic physical or mental illness, and public sinners, such as prostitutes and tax collectors.

Family dynamics

What about family roles? Men are responsible for supporting the family, enforcing social norms within the family, engaging in public life and decision making, and maintaining religious institutions. Women are responsible for running their households, bearing and raising children (to ensure the future of the family), and guarding their sexual purity. Not surprisingly, men hold more rights than women, whose legal rights flow through their closest male relation.

Children are highly valued. They begin helping with adult work as soon as they are able. Basic literacy and numeracy are taught at home by parents, with boys also attending synagogue school. Watch out for children's toys lying around, including child-sized clay vessels (made by the children for practice) and small clay disks used as spinning toys (you will learn more about children in reading guide #24, "Jesus and the Little Children," page 129).

Home sweet home

As you walk with Jesus, you will find yourself in the houses of his friends and followers. Be sure to take off your shoes and wash your feet before entering the house — it is considered polite!

The homes of the poor are usually small, square buildings made of sun-dried mud bricks covered with a waterproof plaster. The interior is usually divided into a raised living area and a lower level for the household animals; these are left outside during the day but brought inside at night.

More often, the houses you visit will feature four or more rooms surrounding a central courtyard. Most houses will be a single level, although the wealthy sometimes build houses of two or three stories. The windows on the lower level are small and placed high on the walls, so the interior is usually dim; you may find clay olive oil lamps burning inside even during the day. The courtyard serves as a kind of combination kitchen, workshop, and living room. It is where most of the cooking is done, usually on an open fire or in an earthen oven. The stone stairs you see in the courtyard lead to the nearly flat roof, which is made of light wooden beams and straw thatch mixed with mud. The roof serves as an outdoor storage space, as well as a place to sleep on hot nights.

The furnishings inside most homes are simple: a few chests for storing clothing; clay vessels for storing wine, grain, and other perishable food; a small metal stove for burning charcoal in cold weather; and maybe a low dining table — although a mat might also serve that purpose. Tables and chairs are uncommon in most homes (wood is scarce, especially in Judah), although they appear in the Roman-style homes of the rich. Expect to sit on mats or cushions on the floor, which is probably going to be packed earth.

Household objects you might see include clay pots, plates, amphoras (tall jars with two handles), and lamps; a loom for weaving cloth; stone mills for pressing olives and milling grain; and trade tools, such as needles or fishing nets.

If you are invited into the home of a wealthy person, you can expect a large, finely constructed building with multiple rooms — vestibules, pantries, cellars, kitchens, and mikves, or ritual baths; you might even find rudimentary indoor plumbing. Mosaics with floral and geometric designs may decorate the floors and walls. Such homes are likely to be filled with fine ceramic and metal vessels, as well as the best wood and stone furnishings.

Won't you stay for supper?

If you stay for a meal, expect a leisurely "slow food" dining experience. You will recline on the floor, with the food spread out on a mat or low platform. Be sure to wash your hands before the meal — it is considered polite, since everyone eats out of common serving dishes, using their bare hands or pieces of bread as a sort of spoon.

Expect Mediterranean cuisine: lots of flatbread, olive oil, spices, fish, fruits, lentils, beans, nuts, dates, figs, grapes, and fruitcakes. No pizza, pasta, tomatoes, potatoes, or chicken, though — those will not come for many more centuries. You will learn more about a typical feast when you join Jesus at a wedding in the village of Cana (reading guide #8, page 63).

If you stay overnight, your host will provide you with a sleeping mat (rolled up and stored away during the day). You will use your cloak for a blanket (you *did* remember to bring your cloak, didn't you?).

Synagogues: Not just for worship

During your travels with Jesus, you are going to visit a lot of synagogues. Synagogues are places of worship, with readings from the Torah and the prophets playing a central role in the service. But they are also an all-purpose gathering place for the local Jewish community; they serve as schools, courtrooms, hostels, meeting rooms, and more. Many first-century synagogues are simple buildings with a large open space for gathering. Inside, you may find benches along the walls, a portable reading platform, and other furnishings and decorations.

The synagogue is often the most important — and prominent — building in a Jewish town. Unlike the Temple, virtually anyone can enter the synagogue, and any man — not just priests or rabbis — can lead the service, reading from and commenting on the Scriptures.

• • •

Now that you have a basic picture of the most common features of biblical Palestine, it is time to venture out on your own. You can read the ensuing forty Gospel stories in order, following a rough timeline of Jesus' ministry. Or you can jump around or use one of the reading plans found on pages 225–234 of this book.

However you proceed, remember to bring your curiosity, an open heart, and a vivid imagination. And above all, always look to Jesus.

(1)

Mary Visits Elizabeth

(Lk 1:39–49)

Walk (or in this case, bounce?) with the baby Jesus as
Mary embarks on a long journey to visit her relative
Elizabeth, who is also expecting a special child.

Prepare

Take a few moments to quietly welcome God's presence.

Lord, thank you for meeting me here in prayer. Thank you for loving me. Please give me the grace to love and serve you in all my thoughts, words, and actions.

Jesus, let me walk with you and Mary to visit your servants Elizabeth, Zechariah, and John. Let your Spirit breathe in me, enlivening my imagination so that I can grow closer to you. Amen.

Read

LUKE 1:39–49

In those days Mary set out and went with haste to a Judean town in the hill country, where she entered the house of Zechariah and greeted Elizabeth. When Elizabeth heard Mary's greeting, the child leaped in her womb. And Elizabeth was filled with the Holy Spirit and exclaimed with a loud cry, "Blessed are you among women, and blessed is the fruit of your womb. And why has this happened to me, that the mother of my Lord comes to me? For as soon as I heard the sound of your greeting, the child in my womb leaped for joy. And blessed is she who believed that there would be a fulfillment of what was spoken to her by the Lord."

And Mary said,
"My soul magnifies the Lord,
    and my spirit rejoices in God my Savior,
for he has looked with favor on the lowliness of his servant.

Surely, from now on all generations will call me blessed;
for the Mighty One has done great things for me,
    and holy is his name."

✠

Set the Scene

To better appreciate this story, recall the story that immediately precedes it. In that passage (Lk 1:26–38), the angel Gabriel appears to Mary to announce that she will bear the Son of God and that her relative Elizabeth is also expecting a child through the providence of God (Lk 1:36–37). Mary sets out to visit Elizabeth, with whom she stays for three months.

Tradition has long held that John the Baptist was born in a little town called Ein Karem located about five miles southwest of ancient Jerusalem. If this was Mary's destination, it would have required a journey of nearly one hundred miles, leading some commentators to speculate that Joseph must have accompanied her, probably returning to his workshop immediately after seeing her safely to her destination.

The text says that the joyful greeting between the two women took place after Mary entered Elizabeth's house, but generations of artists have portrayed the encounter as taking place outdoors. The first Christians would have recognized Mary's song of praise as echoing Hannah's prayer in 1 Samuel 2:1–10. It is also in the tradition of other songs with political overtones sung by Miriam, Deborah, and Judith elsewhere in the Old Testament.

Mary would have stayed in the home of Elizabeth and Zechariah during her three-month visit. Zechariah was a priest of the Temple, so he had a privileged status. Recall, however, that he fell mute after doubting the message of the archangel Gabriel (Lk 1:18–20). He remained mute until the birth of John (Lk 1:57–80), which Mary may have been present for.

Consider ...

- Who are you in this story? Mary? Elizabeth? A traveling companion? A servant in Zechariah's house? Someone else?
- Imagine the greeting between the two women. Where does that take place? What do you see, hear, and feel? Who else is around? What expressions animate the women's faces as they greet each other?
- How is Jesus present to you in this story?
- You might choose to focus on just part of this story: the journey to Elizabeth's house; the meeting of Mary and Elizabeth; or the three months that Mary stays with her and Zechariah.

Walk with Jesus

Take a moment to pray for what your heart most desires from this encounter with Jesus.

Then let the Holy Spirit be your guide as you enter the Gospel story. As you finish walking with Jesus, share your thoughts, feelings, and desires with God, much as one friend would speak to another.

Reflect on the Journey

After you are finished praying, savor and reflect on your experience, either in your prayer journal or with your prayer group. Begin by writing or sharing the story of your imaginative prayer journey: What happened during your time with Jesus? Then consider the following questions:

- Mary and Elizabeth are quite literally pregnant with the fulfillment of God's promise. How are you also "pregnant" with God's plans?
- Mary's Magnificat, her great proclamation of praise, takes up much of this story. Do you ever feel moved to praise God? If so, what moves you, and what does your praise sound like?
- Mary and Elizabeth are spiritual "soul mates." Have you ever bonded with someone over a unique experience in your life? Who is your spiritual soul mate ... or if you don't have one now, can you imagine one?

$$\left(2\right)$$

The Birth of Jesus

(Lk 2:1–20)

Accompany Mary and Joseph as they travel to
Bethlehem, where Jesus will be born.

Prepare

Take a few moments to quietly welcome God's presence.

Lord, thank you for meeting me here in prayer. Thank you for loving me. Please give me the grace to love and serve you in all my thoughts, words, and actions.

Jesus, allow me to welcome your birth alongside the shepherds of Bethlehem. Let your Spirit breathe in me, enlivening my imagination so that I can grow closer to you. Amen.

Read

LUKE 2:1–20

In those days a decree went out from Emperor Augustus that all the world should be registered. This was the first registration and was taken while Quirinius was governor of Syria. All went to their own towns to be registered. Joseph also went from the town of Nazareth in Galilee to Judea, to the city of David called Bethlehem, because he was descended from the house and family of David. He went to be registered with Mary, to whom he was engaged and who was expecting a child. While they were there, the time came for her to deliver her child. And she gave birth to her firstborn son and wrapped him in bands of cloth, and laid him in a manger, because there was no place for them in the inn.

In that region there were shepherds living in the fields, keeping watch over their flock by night. Then an angel of the Lord stood before them, and the glory of the Lord shone around them, and they were terrified. But the angel said to them, "Do not be afraid; for see — I am bringing you good news of great joy for all the people: to you is born this day in the city of David a Savior, who is the Messiah, the Lord. This will be a sign for you: you will find a child wrapped in bands of cloth and lying in a manger." And suddenly there was with the angel a multitude of the heavenly host, praising God and saying,

"Glory to God in the highest heaven,
    and on earth peace among those whom he favors!"

When the angels had left them and gone into heaven, the shepherds said to one another, "Let us go now to Bethlehem and see this thing that has taken place, which the Lord has made known to us." So they went with haste and found Mary and Joseph, and the child lying in the manger. When they saw this, they made known what had been told them about this child; and all who heard it were amazed at what the shepherds told them. But Mary treasured all these words and pondered them in her heart. The shepherds returned, glorifying and praising God for all they had heard and seen, as it had been told them.

✠

Set the Scene

As the story of Jesus' birth opens, Emperor Caesar Augustus (who ruled from 27 B.C. to A.D. 14) appears to be the primary mover and shaker, bringing order to the known world by calling for a census. Caesar Augustus is famous for inaugurating a period of peace within the Roman Empire (the *pax Augusta*). However, his edict becomes the means by which God's plan is fulfilled: It causes Joseph to travel to his ancestral home, where the *real* bringer of peace is born.

The journey from Nazareth to Bethlehem was about ninety miles: south through the forested valley of the Jordan River, with its lions, bears, wild boars, and bandits, and then west through the hill country. The journey may have lasted a week. The weather during the winter months would have been cold (with daytime highs in the 30s and 40s Fahrenheit) and rainy.

Bethlehem, located about five miles south of Jerusalem in the Judean hill country, was built on top of a large aquifer that made the whole region particularly fertile, with abundant almond and olive trees. The town was fortified to protect a large man-made reservoir.

According to early Christian writers, Jesus was born in a cave just outside the village. The cave would have been attached to the inn, providing shelter to donkeys and other pack animals, and serving as "overflow" accommodations for travelers when the inn was full. Mary and Joseph may have shared the space with other travelers; regardless, Mary almost certainly would have received assistance from other women during and immediately after the birth of her child.

Consider ...

- Who are you in this story? You could be Mary, Joseph, one of their traveling companions, the innkeeper, a midwife.
- Imagine the setting of Jesus' birth. What do you see, hear, smell, and feel? What do you see in the faces of the others around you? Can you guess what they might be feeling?
- What do you notice about the newborn Jesus?
- You may wish to focus on just one part of this story: the journey to Bethlehem, the birth of Jesus, or the visitation of the shepherds.

Walk with Jesus

Take a moment to pray for what your heart most desires from this encounter with Jesus.

Then let the Holy Spirit be your guide as you enter the Gospel story.

As you finish walking with Jesus, share your thoughts, feelings, and desires with God, much as one friend would speak to another.

Reflect on the Journey

After you are finished praying, savor and reflect on your experience, either in your prayer journal or with your prayer group. Begin by writing or sharing the story of your imaginative prayer journey: What happened during your time with Jesus? Then consider the following questions:

- What did the journey to Bethlehem require of you?
- Did you hold the baby Jesus? If so, what did you say to him, or to Mary and Joseph? What did he "say" to you?
- The shepherds respond to the birth of Jesus with great

fear at first, and later, with amazement. What emotions or feelings has Jesus stirred in you?

(3)

Following the Star
of the Messiah

(Mt 2:1–12)

Journey with astrologers from a faraway land as they seek
the king announced by a new star in the night sky.

Prepare

Take a few moments to quietly welcome God's presence.

Lord, thank you for meeting me here in prayer. Thank you for loving me. Please give me the grace to love and serve you in all my thoughts, words, and actions.

Jesus, let me join the Magi in seeking you. Let your Spirit breathe in me, enlivening my imagination so that I can grow closer to you. Amen.

Read

MATTHEW 2:1–12

In the time of King Herod, after Jesus was born in Bethlehem of Judea, wise men from the East came to Jerusalem, asking, "Where is the child who has been born king of the Jews? For we observed his star at its rising, and have come to pay him homage." When King Herod heard this, he was frightened, and all Jerusalem with him; and calling together all the chief priests and scribes of the people, he inquired of them where the Messiah was to be born. They told him, "In Bethlehem of Judea; for so it has been written by the prophet:

'And you, Bethlehem, in the land of Judah,
      are by no means least among the rulers of Judah;
    for from you shall come a ruler
      who is to shepherd my people Israel.'"

Then Herod secretly called for the wise men and learned from them the exact time when the star had appeared. Then he sent them to Bethlehem, saying, "Go and search diligently for the child; and when you have found him, bring me word so that I may also go and pay him homage." When they had heard the king, they set out; and there, ahead of them, went the star that they had seen at its rising, until it stopped over the place where the child was. When they saw that the star had stopped, they were overwhelmed with joy. On entering the house, they saw the child with Mary his mother; and they knelt down and paid him homage. Then, opening their treasure chests, they offered him gifts of gold, frankincense, and myrrh. And having been warned in a dream not to return to Herod, they left for their own country by another road.

✠

Set the Scene

Magi were Persian religious figures who practiced astrology; they believed that by studying the movement of the stars, they could understand or predict human events. At the time of Jesus' birth, astrology was considered a science, and astrologers were respected figures in many cultures.

The Gospel does not say how many Magi visited the baby Jesus; today, Western traditions of Christianity usually depict three "wise men," but other traditions have envisioned as many as several dozen.

Given the difficulties of travel in Jesus' time, the Magi probably traveled with supplies, pack animals, and a "support team" to provide security, take care of the animals, and prepare food.

Herod's palace was large enough to receive hundreds of guests. Each of its two main buildings had its own banquet hall, baths, and guest rooms. The center of the palace was filled with gardens, porticoes, fruit groves, canals, and bronze fountains.

The Gospel of Matthew says the Magi found the baby Jesus and his family in a house in Bethlehem. See "A Brief Tour of First-Century Palestine" for a description of what this house may have looked like.

Consider …

- Who are you in this story? You could be one of the Magi or a servant in their caravan, an official of King Herod's court, a neighbor.
- What do you see, hear, and smell? What details do you notice in Herod's palace? How about in the house where the Holy Family is staying? What is the light like?
- What do you notice about the baby Jesus? How do you feel toward him?

Walk with Jesus

Take a moment to pray for what your heart most desires from this encounter with Jesus.

Then let the Holy Spirit be your guide as you enter the Gospel story.

As you finish walking with Jesus, share your thoughts, feelings, and desires with God, much as one friend would speak to another.

Reflect on the Journey

After you are finished praying, savor and reflect on your experience, either in your prayer journal or with your prayer group. Begin by writing or sharing the story of your imaginative prayer journey: What happened during your time with Jesus? Then consider the following questions:

- Do you ever feel provoked by Jesus as King Herod did?
- "On entering the house, they saw the child with Mary his mother; and they knelt down and paid him homage" (Mt. 2:11). How did you approach the infant Jesus? How did you feel?
- What gifts do you bring to Jesus today?

(4)

The Holy Family
Flees to Egypt

(Mt 2:13–15, 19–21)

Journey with Jesus as he and his family flee
their home to find refuge in Egypt.

Prepare

Take a few moments to quietly welcome God's presence.

Lord, thank you for meeting me here in prayer. Thank you for loving me. Please give me the grace to love and serve you in all my thoughts, words, and actions.

Jesus, let me travel with you as a refugee in a foreign land. Let your Spirit breathe in me, enlivening my imagination so that I can grow closer to you. Amen.

Read

MATTHEW 2:13–15, 19–21
Now after they had left, an angel of the Lord appeared to Joseph in a dream and said, "Get up, take the child and his mother, and flee to Egypt, and remain there until I tell you; for Herod is about to search for the child, to destroy him." Then Joseph got up, took the child and his mother by night, and went to Egypt, and remained there until the death of Herod. This was to fulfill what had been spoken by the Lord through the prophet, "Out of Egypt I have called my son."

When Herod died, an angel of the Lord suddenly appeared in a dream to Joseph in Egypt and said, "Get up, take the child and his mother, and go to the land of Israel, for those who were seeking the child's life are dead." Then Joseph got up, took the child and his mother, and went to the land of Israel.

✠

Set the Scene

The journey to Egypt would have taken Joseph, Mary, and the child Jesus about two weeks. The most common route passed through cities and towns along the coast of the Mediterranean Sea.

Egypt in the first century was a province of the Roman Empire, and one of the richest outside of Italy. The fertile soils of the Nile Delta produced most of the grain for the empire, and supported large metropolitan cities bustling with trade, such as Alexandria and Memphis. Alexandria's population is estimated to have been about one million at its peak. Native Egyptians populated the rural areas, working as peasant farmers.

Whether the family settled in a large city or a small farming village, as foreigners, they would have depended on the charity of other Jews. Fortunately, there were large communities of Jews living throughout Egypt.

How long did Jesus live in Egypt with his parents? Based on

the date of King Herod's death, their sojourn would not have been longer than a few years. Whom would Jesus' family have met during their journey? The cities and towns along the coast of the Mediterranean Sea and the banks of the Nile River bustled with people from all over the ancient world — among them Romans, Greeks, native Egyptians, and Jews. The Roman and Greek citizens who made up the urban elite enjoyed special privileges. These differences caused friction between the groups, which sometimes resulted in riots or fighting.

Consider ...

- Who are you in this story? Some options include Mary, Joseph, a fellow traveler, or a welcoming member of the Jewish community in Egypt.
- What do you see, hear, and smell? What strange plants and animals do you see? What types of people do you encounter? What does the food taste like?
- What do you notice about Jesus as a toddler? What catches his attention?
- This passage has many possibilities for imaginative prayer. You might focus on the Holy Family's departure from Palestine, their sojourn in Egypt, or their return to Israel. Try focusing on the events of a few hours in a single day.

Walk with Jesus

Take a moment to pray for what your heart most desires from this encounter with Jesus.

Then let the Holy Spirit be your guide as you enter the Gospel story.

As you finish walking with Jesus, share your thoughts, feelings, and desires with God, much as one friend would speak to another.

Reflect on the Journey

After you are finished praying, savor and reflect on your experience, either in your prayer journal or with your prayer group. Begin by writing or sharing the story of your imaginative prayer journey: What happened during your time with Jesus? Then consider the following questions:

- Joseph is sometimes called "the dreamer" because God spoke to him through four dreams. How does God speak to you?
- How did you interact with Jesus as a toddler? Were you able to help Mary and Joseph care for him?
- Have you ever experienced a sudden disruption or displacement in your life? Where did you find refuge? Where was God?

(5)

The Finding of Jesus in the Temple

(Lk 2:41–51)

Walk with Jesus, now a twelve-year-old boy, as he visits Jerusalem for the weeklong Passover festival — and decides to stay behind when the rest of his family's travel group departs for Nazareth.

Prepare

Take a few moments to quietly welcome God's presence.

Lord, thank you for meeting me here in prayer. Thank you for loving me. Please give me the grace to love and serve you in all my thoughts, words, and actions.

Jesus, allow me to stay with you in your Father's house. Let your Spirit breathe in me, enlivening my imagination so that I can grow closer to you. Amen.

Read

LUKE 2:41–51

Now every year his parents went to Jerusalem for the festival of the Passover. And when he was twelve years old, they went up as usual for the festival. When the festival was ended and they started to return, the boy Jesus stayed behind in Jerusalem, but his parents did not know it. Assuming that he was in the group of travelers, they went a day's journey. Then they started to look for him among their relatives and friends. When they did not find him, they returned to Jerusalem to search for him. After three days they found him in the temple, sitting among the teachers, listening to them and asking them questions. And all who heard him were amazed at his understanding and his answers. When his parents saw him they were astonished; and his mother said to him, "Child, why have you treated us like this? Look, your father and I have been searching for you in great anxiety." He said to them, "Why were you searching for me? Did you not know that I must be in my Father's house?" But they did not understand what he said to them. Then he went down with them and came to Nazareth, and was obedient to them. His mother treasured all these things in her heart.

✠

Set the Scene

To better imagine the Holy Family's experience in Jerusalem during the Passover festival, see "A Brief Tour of First-Century Palestine," which also describes the busy Temple area.

Note that the family traveled to and from Jerusalem in a caravan with relatives and friends, some of whom undoubtedly helped Mary and Joseph search for their child. They would have had a difficult time finding Jesus in the Temple: Tens of thousands of people would have filled the complex, with its numerous courts, porches, porticoes, and buildings. When they did find him, he may have been on one of the upper floors of the Royal Porch, where the most learned rabbis gathered.

Consider ...

- Who are you in this story? You could be one of the teachers in the Temple, one of Mary and Joseph's relatives or friends, someone who feeds and shelters Jesus during his three-day stay in Jerusalem.
- What sights, sounds, or smells most impress you in the Temple area? Who are some of the people Jesus meets during his time in the Temple? What do they look like?
- What do you notice about Jesus as he interacts with the teachers? How do you feel toward him?

Walk with Jesus

Take a moment to pray for what your heart most desires from this encounter with Jesus.

Then let the Holy Spirit be your guide as you enter the Gospel story.

As you finish walking with Jesus, share your thoughts, feelings, and desires with God, much as one friend would speak to another.

Reflect on the Journey

After you are finished praying, savor and reflect on your experience, either in your prayer journal or with your prayer group. Begin by writing or sharing the story of your imaginative prayer journey: What happened during your time with Jesus? Then consider the following questions:

- What was it like searching for Jesus with Mary and

Joseph?
- Have you ever felt as though you "lost" Jesus? What was that time like? How did you find him again?
- The wisest teachers of Israel were astounded at the wisdom of the boy Jesus. What wisdom has the child Jesus taught you?
- Have you ever wanted to say to Jesus, "Why have you done this to me?"

(6)

John Baptizes Jesus
in the Jordan River

(Mk 1:4–11)

Walk with Jesus as he wades into the Jordan River
to seek baptism from John the Baptist.

Prepare

Take a few moments to quietly welcome God's presence.

Lord, thank you for meeting me here in prayer. Thank you for loving me. Please give me the grace to love and serve you in all my thoughts, words, and actions.

Jesus, let me join you among the crowds on the banks of the Jordan River. Let your Spirit breathe in me, enlivening my imagination so that I can grow closer to you. Amen.

Read

MARK 1:4–11

John the baptizer appeared in the wilderness, proclaiming a baptism of repentance for the forgiveness of sins. And people from the whole Judean countryside and all the people of Jerusalem were going out to him, and were baptized by him in the river Jordan, confessing their sins. Now John was clothed with camel's hair, with a leather belt around his waist, and he ate locusts and wild honey. He proclaimed, "The one who is more powerful than I is coming after me; I am not worthy to stoop down and untie the thong of his sandals. I have baptized you with water; but he will baptize you with the Holy Spirit."

In those days Jesus came from Nazareth of Galilee and was baptized by John in the Jordan. And just as he was coming up out of the water, he saw the heavens torn apart and the Spirit descending like a dove on him. And a voice came from heaven, "You are my Son, the Beloved; with you I am well pleased."

✠

Set the Scene

Qasr el Yahud, the traditional site of Jesus' baptism on the Jordan River, is about twenty-five miles east of Jerusalem — usually a journey of about two days for the people of Jesus' time. The river is small, no wider than a hundred feet across. Although it is surrounded by a dry, empty desert, its banks are green with small trees, bushes, and grasses.

The Jordan River held a special place in the memory of Israel; Joshua parted its waters when Israel first entered the Promised Land (Jos 3:1–17), and the prophet Elisha cured Naaman of his leprosy by having him bathe in its waters (2 Kgs 5:1–19). Its waters were used for purification rituals.

According to the Gospel of Luke, John preached charity toward the poor and baptized anyone who came to him — even tax collectors and soldiers. His simple clothing reminded people of the clothing worn by the prophet Elijah. According to the Jewish historian Josephus, John was so popular, King Herod worried that the people would do whatever he said — even start a rebellion.

Consider ...
- Who are you in this story? One of the disciples of John? A follower of Jesus? Someone in the crowd?
- Imagine the scene on the banks of the Jordan River. What do you see, hear, and feel? How far did you have to travel to get to the river? What did you need along the way? What other details do you notice — the weather, the noise of the crowd, the smell of the land?
- What do you notice about Jesus as he emerges from the water?

Walk with Jesus
Take a moment to pray for what your heart most desires from this encounter with Jesus.

Then let the Holy Spirit be your guide as you enter the Gospel story.

As you finish walking with Jesus, share your thoughts, feelings, and desires with God, much as one friend would speak to another.

Reflect on the Journey
After you are finished praying, savor and reflect on your experience, either in your prayer journal or with your prayer group. Begin by writing or sharing the story of your imaginative prayer journey: What happened during your time with Jesus? Then consider the following questions:

- "Repent, for the kingdom of heaven has come near" (Mt 3:2). Do John's words stir your heart? If so, how?

- Jesus' baptism in the Jordan marks the beginning of his public ministry. What event or ritual marked the beginning of a new chapter in your life? Where was God in that?
- What would it be like to hear God call you "beloved"?

$$\left(7 \right)$$

The Miraculous
Catch of Fish

(Lk 5:3–11)

Walk with Jesus as he calls Peter, James, and John to follow
him ... after producing a miraculous catch of fish.

Prepare
Take a few moments to quietly welcome God's presence.

Lord, thank you for meeting me here in prayer. Thank you for loving me. Please give me the grace to love and serve you in all my
thoughts, words, and actions.

Jesus, may I walk with you along the shore of the Sea of Galilee as you call your first followers. Let your Spirit breathe in me,
enlivening my imagination so that I can grow closer to you. Amen.

Read

LUKE 5:3–11

He got into one of the boats, the one belonging to Simon, and asked him to put out a little way from the shore. Then he sat down and taught the crowds from the boat. When he had finished speaking, he said to Simon, "Put out into the deep water and let down your nets for a catch." Simon answered, "Master, we have worked all night long but have caught nothing. Yet if you say so, I will let down the nets." When they had done this, they caught so many fish that their nets were beginning to break. So they signaled their partners in the other boat to come and help them. And they came and filled both boats, so that they began to sink. But when Simon Peter saw it, he fell down at Jesus' knees, saying, "Go away from me, Lord, for I am a sinful man!" For he and all who were with him were amazed at the catch of fish that they had taken; and so also were James and John, sons of Zebedee, who were partners with Simon. Then Jesus said to Simon, "Do not be afraid; from now on you will be catching people." When they had brought their boats to shore, they left everything and followed him.

✠

Set the Scene

This story takes place near Capernaum on the Lake of Gennesaret (the Sea of Galilee), on whose shores much of Jesus' ministry took place. The lake was well known for its rich fisheries; hundreds of fishing operations exported salted fish throughout the region. Those who owned their own fishing boats on the lake would probably have been relatively affluent.

Simon and his brother Andrew (unnamed in this reading) were originally from the nearby village of Bethsaida, although by the time of Jesus' ministry, they resided in Capernaum. They were business partners with the sons of Zebedee, James and John.

If they were successful at their trade, Simon and his partners were probably hard-working, persistent, patient, and detail orient-ed. Fishermen put in long hours year-round, in all sorts of weather; they often worked at night, when the fish were less likely to avoid the nets in the dark. The nets were handmade of linen; depending on the type, they might also feature cork floaters and stone weights. They were either thrown from shore or, as in this story, dropped into the deep water several hundred yards offshore.

The nets had to be repaired and cleaned after every fishing trip to prevent them from rotting — a major chore, given that they were hundreds of feet long. So, when Jesus encounters Simon and his partners cleaning the nets on the shore, they probably had hours of work ahead of them, despite having spent all night on the water.

Consider …

- Who are you in this story? One of the fishermen? Someone in the crowd listening to Jesus?
- What do you smell and hear along the shore of the lake? What is the weather like? What do you notice about Simon's mood and facial expressions as this story unfolds?
- What do you notice about Jesus? What is his demeanor like when he tells Peter to go back out on the water? How does he react to the large catch of fish?

Walk with Jesus

Take a moment to pray for what your heart most desires from this encounter with Jesus.

Then let the Holy Spirit be your guide as you enter the Gospel story.

As you finish walking with Jesus, share your thoughts, feelings, and desires with God, much as one friend would speak to another.

Reflect on the Journey

After you are finished praying, savor and reflect on your experience, either in your prayer journal or with your prayer group. Begin by writing or sharing the story of your imaginative prayer journey: What happened during your time with Jesus? Then consider the following questions:

- How would you react if Jesus asked you to change what you were doing or try something new?
- "Go away from me, Lord, for I am a sinful man" (Lk 5:8). Like Peter, have you ever wanted Jesus to depart from you?
- What kind of work do you do? What skills do you have that Jesus might want to use in his mission?

(8)

The Wedding at Cana

(Jn 2:1–10)

Join Jesus and his disciples as they attend
a wedding in the village of Cana.

Prepare

Take a few moments to quietly welcome God's presence.

Lord, thank you for meeting me here in prayer. Thank you for loving me. Please give me the grace to love and serve you in all my thoughts, words, and actions.

Jesus, let me join you and your friends as you attend the wedding at Cana. Let your Spirit breathe in me, enlivening my imagination so that I can grow closer to you. Amen.

Read

JOHN 2:1–10

On the third day there was a wedding in Cana of Galilee, and the mother of Jesus was there. Jesus and his disciples had also been invited to the wedding. When the wine gave out, the mother of Jesus said to him, "They have no wine." And Jesus said to her, "Woman, what concern is that to you and to me? My hour has not yet come." His mother said to the servants, "Do whatever he tells you."

Now standing there were six stone water jars for the Jewish rites of purification, each holding twenty or thirty gallons. Jesus said to them, "Fill the jars with water." And they filled them up to the brim. He said to them, "Now draw some out, and take it to the chief steward." So they took it. When the steward tasted the water that had become wine, and did not know where it came from (though the servants who had drawn the water knew), the steward called the bridegroom and said to him, "Everyone serves the good wine first, and then the inferior wine after the guests have become drunk. But you have kept the good wine until now."

✠

Set the Scene

This story takes place "on the third day" after John the Baptist testifies to Jesus (Jn 1:32–34) and immediately after the account of Jesus' calling the apostles. The location of Cana is disputed among scholars, but it was probably a relatively small village somewhere in Galilee. Jesus attends the wedding in the company of his disciples as well as his mother and other relatives.

Jewish weddings were big celebrations lasting five to seven days, full of rituals, blessings, music, dancing, games, and food. Usually, the entire village would attend. Weddings were often held in the autumn, to coincide with the harvest.

The first day would feature a procession in which the bride, veiled and dressed in the finest clothes and jewelry her family could afford, would be carried in a canopied litter to the groom's house. The groom would also be dressed splendidly. The bride and her friends would retire to a separate room while the groom and the other guests celebrated.

The next day featured the wedding feast, during which the men and women were served separately. The bride sat under a canopy, surrounded by her bridesmaids, while songs were sung and blessings were said. Later that evening, the groom joined the bride under the canopy, and a blessing was said over the couple. The men and women guests would come together for the evening feast. The marriage would be consummated later that evening, but the celebration would continue for several more days.

Besides wine, the guests would have enjoyed goat cheese, the meat of sheep and goats (or cattle, if the couple were wealthy), fish, poultry (ducks, geese, pigeons — but not chickens, which had not been domesticated yet), various kinds of bread, lentils, almonds, beans, dates, figs, melons, grapes, and fruitcakes. Food would have been eaten from a common dish.

Some commentators have speculated that the wedding couple may have been relatives of Mary, which would account for her special concern about the wine running out.

Consider ...

- Who are you in this story? Are you a friend or relative of the bride and groom? Are you one of the happy couple?
- Imagine the setting of this wedding celebration. Where does it take place? What do the food and drink smell and taste like? What do the music and singing sound like? How is the place decorated?
- What do you notice about Jesus? How does he participate in the celebration? What about Mary?

Walk with Jesus

Take a moment to pray for what your heart most desires from this encounter with Jesus.

Then let the Holy Spirit be your guide as you enter the Gospel story.

As you finish walking with Jesus, share your thoughts, feelings, and desires with God, much as one friend would speak to another.

Reflect on the Journey

After you are finished praying, savor and reflect on your experience, either in your prayer journal or with your prayer group. Begin by writing or sharing the story of your imaginative prayer journey: What happened during your time with Jesus? Then consider the following questions:

- What was it like to celebrate with Jesus and Mary? Do you feel that Jesus celebrates with you at the important milestones in your life?
- Jesus seems to refuse his mother's request at first. Have you ever had a similar experience in prayer? If so, how did you respond?
- "Do whatever he tells you" (Jn 2:5). How do you respond to these words from Mary?

(9)

A Busy Day in Capernaum

(Mk 1:29–39)

Walk with Jesus as he visits Simon Peter's house in
Capernaum, healing the sick who seek him out.

Prepare
Take a few moments to quietly welcome God's presence.

Lord, thank you for meeting me here in prayer. Thank you for loving me. Please give me the grace to love and serve you in all my
thoughts, words, and actions.

Jesus, let me accompany you as you visit Simon's house in
Capernaum. Let your Spirit breathe in me, enlivening my imagination so that I can grow closer to you. Amen.

Read

MARK 1:29–39

As soon as they left the synagogue, they entered the house of Simon and Andrew, with James and John. Now Simon's mother-in-law was in bed with a fever, and they told him about her at once. He came and took her by the hand and lifted her up. Then the fever left her, and she began to serve them.

That evening, at sunset, they brought to him all who were sick or possessed with demons. And the whole city was gathered around the door. And he cured many who were sick with various diseases, and cast out many demons; and he would not permit the demons to speak, because they knew him.

In the morning, while it was still very dark, he got up and went out to a deserted place, and there he prayed. And Simon and his companions hunted for him. When they found him, they said to him, "Everyone is searching for you." He answered, "Let us go on to the neighboring towns, so that I may proclaim the message there also; for that is what I came out to do." And he went throughout Galilee, proclaiming the message in their synagogues and casting out demons.

✠

Set the Scene

The story opens with Jesus returning to Capernaum, a fishing village of about 1,500 people on the northern shore of the Sea of Galilee. See "A Brief Tour of First-Century Palestine" for more about Capernaum.

In recent decades, archaeologists have uncovered a house that they believe was Peter's house in Capernaum, based on the fact that the otherwise ordinary dwelling underwent dramatic transformations around the time of Jesus' death, eventually becoming a church that was a pilgrimage site for centuries. This house was part of a complex of similar dwellings, located about halfway between the synagogue and the shore of the Sea of Galilee, only a few hundred feet away. See "A Brief Tour of First-Century Palestine" for more about what first-century houses looked like.

For the people of the first-century Mediterranean world, being sick and being demon-possessed were closely related phenomena. Being sick wasn't just a physical disorder, but a spiritual one too — a manifestation of evil. Jesus' healing ministry, like his casting out of demons, demonstrated his spiritual authority.

Although the people seeking Jesus' healing dominate this story, notice two other moments in this account: Jesus and his friends being served by Simon's mother-in-law, and Jesus getting up before dawn to pray in a quiet place.

Consider ...

- Who are you in this story? You could be Peter's mother-in-law, one of the sick, a follower of Jesus, or just a curious onlooker.
- Imagine Peter's house. What do you see, hear, and smell? What kind of people come to Jesus for healing? What are their sicknesses or infirmities?
- What do you notice about Jesus' hands and eyes as he heals each person? How do you feel toward him?

Walk with Jesus

Take a moment to pray for what your heart most desires from this encounter with Jesus.

Then let the Holy Spirit be your guide as you enter the Gospel story.

As you finish walking with Jesus, share your thoughts, feelings, and desires with God, much as one friend would speak to another.

Reflect on the Journey

After you are finished praying, savor and reflect on your experience, either in your prayer journal or with your prayer group. Begin by writing or sharing the story of your imaginative prayer journey: What happened during your time with Jesus? Then consider the following questions:

- In this story, Simon experiences Jesus hard at work helping others, enjoying a meal in the company of friends, and in quiet prayer. What is your favorite way to spend time with Jesus?
- How do you feel about approaching Jesus for healing?
- Do you ever feel like Jesus, beset by the crush of other people's needs? Do you ever feel the need to get away, as Jesus did?

(10)

Jesus Heals a Paralyzed Man

(Mk 2:1–12)

Walk with Jesus as he heals a man paralyzed from birth.

Prepare

Take a few moments to quietly welcome God's presence.

Lord, thank you for meeting me here in prayer. Thank you for loving me. Please give me the grace to love and serve you in all my thoughts, words, and actions.

Jesus, may I walk with you as you forgive sins and heal people in Peter's house. Let your Spirit breathe in me, enlivening my imagination so that I can grow closer to you. Amen.

Read

MARK 2:1–12

When he returned to Capernaum after some days, it was reported that he was at home. So many gathered around that there was no longer room for them, not even in front of the door; and he was speaking the word to them. Then some people came, bringing to him a paralyzed man, carried by four of them. And when they could not bring him to Jesus because of the crowd, they removed the roof above him; and after having dug through it, they let down the mat on which the paralytic lay. When Jesus saw their faith, he said to the paralytic, "Son, your sins are forgiven." Now some of the scribes were sitting there, questioning in their hearts, "Why does this fellow speak in this way? It is blasphemy! Who can forgive sins but God alone?" At once Jesus perceived in his spirit that they were discussing these questions among themselves; and he said to them, "Why do you raise such questions in your hearts? Which is easier, to say to the paralytic, 'Your sins are forgiven,' or to say, 'Stand up and take your mat and walk'? But so that you may know that the Son of Man has authority on earth to forgive sins" — he said to the paralytic — "I say to you, stand up, take your mat and go to your home." And he stood up, and immediately took the mat and went out before all of them; so that they were all amazed and glorified God, saying, "We have never seen anything like this!"

✠

Set the Scene

Among those present in the large crowd that gathers to see Jesus in Capernaum are some scribes, expert writers responsible for copying the Scriptures and drafting legal contracts. They were regarded as legal experts qualified to pass judgment on how the law should be lived out in everyday life.

Disability and chronic sickness were widely regarded as part of God's punishment for sin — either one's own or one's parents'.

The house where Jesus stayed may have been Peter's. The roof was probably made of light beams and straw thatch mixed with mud, which hardened into a clay, so you can imagine chunks of mud and straw falling into the crowd below as the paralytic's friends opened a hole in it.

Consider ...

- Who are you in this story? You could be the paralytic, one of his friends who carry him to Jesus, someone in the crowd, or even one of the scribes.
- Imagine the crowded house where Jesus is preaching. Think about where you stand: Are you inside the house with Jesus, or outside with the crowd, or on the rooftop? What sound does the crowd make when the man stands?
- What do you notice about Jesus? What does he do? How does his mood and demeanor change as the story unfolds?

Walk with Jesus

Take a moment to pray for what your heart most desires from this encounter with Jesus.

Then let the Holy Spirit be your guide as you enter the Gospel story.

As you finish walking with Jesus, share your thoughts, feelings, and desires with God, much as one friend would speak to another.

Reflect on the Journey

After you are finished praying, savor and reflect on your experience, either in your prayer journal or with your prayer group. Begin by writing or sharing the story of your imaginative prayer journey: What happened during your time with Jesus? Then consider the following questions:

- The people in this story went to great lengths to get to Jesus. Do you ever feel it is difficult to approach Jesus? If so, what stands in your way?
- Have you ever "carried" someone to Jesus to be healed? How?
- What would it be like to hear Jesus tell you that your sins are forgiven?
- Do you ever second-guess Jesus, as the scribes in this story do?

(11)

Jesus Heals the Centurion's Servant

(Mt 8:5–13)

Walk with Jesus as he is approached by a Roman centurion who asks him to heal his servant who is suffering greatly.

Prepare

Take a few moments to quietly welcome God's presence.

Lord, thank you for meeting me here in prayer. Thank you for loving me. Please give me the grace to love and serve you in all my thoughts, words, and actions.

Jesus, allow me to accompany you as you heal the centurion's servant, showing that your mercy has no bounds. Let your Spirit breathe in me, enlivening my imagination so that I can grow closer to you. Amen.

Read

MATTHEW 8:5–13

When he entered Capernaum, a centurion came to him, appealing to him and saying, "Lord, my servant is lying at home paralyzed, in terrible distress." And he said to him, "I will come and cure him." The centurion answered, "Lord, I am not worthy to have you come under my roof; but only speak the word, and my servant will be healed. For I also am a man under authority, with soldiers under me; and I say to one, 'Go,' and he goes, and to another, 'Come,' and he comes, and to my slave, 'Do this,' and the slave does it." When Jesus heard him, he was amazed and said to those who followed him, "Truly I tell you, in no one in Israel have I found such faith. I tell you, many will come from east and west and will eat with Abraham and Isaac and Jacob in the kingdom of heaven, while the heirs of the kingdom will be thrown into the outer darkness, where there will be weeping and gnashing of teeth." And to the centurion Jesus said, "Go; let it be done for you according to your faith." And the servant was healed in that hour.

✠

Set the Scene

Earlier in this chapter of Matthew's Gospel, the author notes that "large crowds" followed Jesus after his Sermon on the Mount. These crowds are with him as he is approached by a Roman centurion, a military officer commanding one hundred men.

The Roman occupying forces were deeply resented by the Jews, although in Luke's telling of this story, the Jewish elders intercede with Jesus on behalf of the centurion, citing his love for the Jewish people (Lk 7:1–10). Still, being directly approached by a centurion would not have been a trivial matter. If you have ever been singled out by an authority figure, you can imagine how Jesus and his companions might have felt.

When the centurion says his servant is suffering greatly, he is probably saying that he is afflicted by demons, the source of his paralysis. It is these demons who will follow Jesus' orders.

Consider ...

- Who are you in this story? Are you the centurion, his servant, one of Jesus' followers, a curious onlooker?
- What do you see, hear, and smell in this story? Where is Jesus exactly as he enters Capernaum? Who is with him, and what do his surroundings look like? Is the centurion alone, or accompanied by others?
- What do you notice about Jesus as he speaks with the centurion?

Walk with Jesus

Take a moment to pray for what your heart most desires from this encounter with Jesus.

Then let the Holy Spirit be your guide as you enter the Gospel story.

As you finish walking with Jesus, share your thoughts, feelings, and desires with God, much as one friend would speak to another.

Reflect on the Journey

After you are finished praying, savor and reflect on your experience, either in your prayer journal or with your prayer group. Begin by writing or sharing the story of your imaginative prayer journey: What happened during your time with Jesus? Then consider the following questions:

- The centurion claims to be a man of authority, and recognizes Jesus as a man with authority, too. How do you feel about authority? What does Jesus have authority over in your life?

- Whom do you know who has the kind of faith displayed by the centurion? How has this person affected your own faith?
- What about you amazes Jesus?

(12)

Jesus Calms the Stormy Sea

(Mk 4:35–41)

Accompany Jesus and his disciples as they cross
the stormy Sea of Galilee in a fishing boat.

Prepare
Take a few moments to quietly welcome God's presence.

Lord, thank you for meeting me here in prayer. Thank you for loving me. Please give me the grace to love and serve you in all my thoughts, words, and actions.

Jesus, let me get in the boat with you and your disciples as you head into stormy seas. Let your Spirit breathe in me, enlivening my imagination so that I can grow closer to you. Amen.

Read

MARK 4:35–41

On that day, when evening had come, he said to them, "Let us go across to the other side." And leaving the crowd behind, they took him with them in the boat, just as he was. Other boats were with him. A great windstorm arose, and the waves beat into the boat, so that the boat was already being swamped. But he was in the stern, asleep on the cushion; and they woke him up and said to him, "Teacher, do you not care that we are perishing?" He woke up and rebuked the wind, and said to the sea, "Peace! Be still!" Then the wind ceased, and there was a dead calm. He said to them, "Why are you afraid? Have you still no faith?" And they were filled with great awe and said to one another, "Who then is this, that even the wind and the sea obey him?"

☩

Set the Scene

It is evening as Jesus asks his followers to cross to the other side of the huge (thirteen miles long by eight miles across) freshwater lake known as the Sea of Galilee. Some of Jesus' disciples were fishermen and expert boatmen, who were very familiar with the lake. But even the fishermen probably couldn't swim, and they usually would have fished within sight of shore. Moreover, the Jewish worldview of the time associated the deep waters of seas and oceans with chaos and monsters.

Being caught in a storm on this huge freshwater lake was no trivial matter, then; wind-whipped waves can reach six feet high. Notice that the text says that waves were actually breaking over the boat.

The disciples and Jesus probably took a typical fishing boat of the time — shallow-drafted and flat-bottomed, about twenty-seven feet long and seven feet wide. It would have had a mast for a sail and oars for rowing. See "A Brief Tour of First-Century Palestine" for more about the Sea of Galilee.

Consider ...
- Who are you in this story? You could be one of the disciples ... or could you stow away as yourself?
- Imagine the small fishing boat in the midst of the stormy sea. What do you see, hear, and feel? What does the sea smell like? Where are you in the boat, and what does it feel like?
- What does Jesus look like as he is sleeping? Do your feelings toward Jesus change over the course of the story?

Walk with Jesus
Take a moment to pray for what your heart most desires from this encounter with Jesus.

Then let the Holy Spirit be your guide as you enter the Gospel story.

As you finish walking with Jesus, share your thoughts, feelings, and desires with God, much as one friend would speak to another.

Reflect on the Journey
After you are finished praying, savor and reflect on your experience, either in your prayer journal or with your prayer group. Begin by writing or sharing the story of your imaginative prayer journey: What happened during your time with Jesus? Then consider the following questions:

- Have you ever felt that Jesus was "in the boat" with you during a time of fear or danger? Did he seem to be "asleep," awake, or actively in control?
- The disciples sound utterly exasperated with Jesus' seeming lack of concern. Do you ever get exasperated with Jesus?
- How do you respond to Jesus' questions about being afraid and lacking faith?

(13)

Jesus Calls Matthew
and Eats with Sinners

(Mt 9:9–13)

Follow Jesus as he eats with social and religious
outcasts in Capernaum … including his newest
disciple, Matthew the tax collector.

Prepare

Take a few moments to quietly welcome God's presence.

Lord, thank you for meeting me here in prayer. Thank you for loving me. Please give me the grace to love and serve you in all my
thoughts, words, and actions.

Jesus, let me be at your side as you socialize with Matthew and
other social outcasts. Let your Spirit breathe in me, enlivening my

imagination so that I can grow closer to you. Amen.

Read

MATTHEW 9:9–13

As Jesus was walking along, he saw a man called Matthew sitting at the tax booth; and he said to him, "Follow me." And he got up and followed him.

And as he sat at dinner in the house, many tax collectors and sinners came and were sitting with him and his disciples. When the Pharisees saw this, they said to his disciples, "Why does your teacher eat with tax collectors and sinners?" But when he heard this, he said, "Those who are well have no need of a physician, but those who are sick. Go and learn what this means, 'I desire mercy, not sacrifice.' For I have come to call not the righteous but sinners."

✠

Set the Scene

The encounter between Jesus and Matthew takes place in Capernaum shortly after Jesus has healed the paralytic on a stretcher (Mt 9:1–8; see reading guide #10, page 71).

Tax collectors were the most despised members of Jewish society, widely considered traitors and thieves. Tax collectors bid for the right to their position; the highest bidder paid a set amount to the Roman authorities, keeping the remainder of what they collected for themselves. So besides collaborating with the Roman occupiers, they also lined their own pockets, adding to the crushing tax burden most Jews experienced.

Matthew collected customs taxes on exports and imports passing through the busy port city of Capernaum. His post would have been located in a high-traffic location, either at the port or along a major thoroughfare. As such, Matthew must have been aware of Jesus' ministry and miracles. In fact, given that several of Jesus' disciples exported fish from Capernaum, they may have had personal dealings with Matthew in his tax-collecting role.

Given his status and wealth, the dinner party Matthew hosted for Jesus, the disciples, and the other tax collectors and sinners probably featured good food and wine, as well as luxurious surroundings.

Consider ...
- Who are you in this story? Matthew, one of the disciples, or a curious bystander? One of the other "tax collectors and sinners" at Matthew's home, or one of the religious officials?
- What do you see, hear, and smell? What do you notice about Matthew's tax booth and its surroundings? What is Matthew like?
- What do you notice about how Jesus approaches Matthew?

Walk with Jesus
Take a moment to pray for what your heart most desires from this encounter with Jesus.

Then let the Holy Spirit be your guide as you enter the Gospel story.

As you finish walking with Jesus, share your thoughts, feelings, and desires with God, much as one friend would speak to another.

Reflect on the Journey
After you are finished praying, savor and reflect on your experience, either in your prayer journal or with your prayer group. Begin by writing or sharing the story of your imaginative prayer journey: What happened during your time with Jesus? Then consider the following questions:

- Have you ever felt like Matthew — despised or rejected?
- What have you given up to follow Jesus?

- If Jesus invited you to a dinner party hosted by a notorious sinner, would you go?

(14)

The Daughter of Jairus and the Woman with a Hemorrhage

(Lk 8:40–56)

Walk with Jesus as he goes to the home of a synagogue official whose daughter is dying and as he encounters a woman who is also desperate for healing.

Prepare

Take a few moments to quietly welcome God's presence.

Lord, thank you for meeting me here in prayer. Thank you for loving me. Please give me the grace to love and serve you in all my thoughts, words, and actions.

Jesus, let me walk with you as you bring hope and healing to those devastated by chronic illness and the death of a child. Let your Spirit breathe in me, enlivening my imagination so that I can grow closer to you. Amen.

Read

LUKE 8:40–56

Now when Jesus returned, the crowd welcomed him, for they were all waiting for him. Just then there came a man named Jairus, a leader of the synagogue. He fell at Jesus' feet and begged him to come to his house, for he had an only daughter, about twelve years old, who was dying.

As he went, the crowds pressed in on him. Now there was a woman who had been suffering from hemorrhages for twelve years; and though she had spent all she had on physicians, no one could cure her. She came up behind him and touched the fringe of his clothes, and immediately her hemorrhage stopped. Then Jesus asked, "Who touched me?" When all denied it, Peter said, "Master, the crowds surround you and press in on you." But Jesus said, "Someone touched me; for I noticed that power had gone out from me." When the woman saw that she could not remain hidden, she came trembling; and falling down before him, she declared in the presence of all the people why she had touched him, and how she had been immediately healed. He said to her, "Daughter, your faith has made you well; go in peace."

While he was still speaking, someone came from the leader's house to say, "Your daughter is dead; do not trouble the teacher any longer." When Jesus heard this, he replied, "Do not fear. Only believe, and she will be saved." When he came to the house, he did not allow anyone to enter with him, except Peter, John, and James, and the child's father and mother. They were all weeping and wailing for her; but he said, "Do not weep; for she is not dead but sleeping." And they laughed at him, knowing that she was dead. But he took her by the hand and called out, "Child, get up!" Her spirit returned, and she got up at once. Then he directed them to give her something to eat. Her parents were astounded; but he ordered them to tell no one what had happened.

✠

Set the Scene

This story follows immediately after the story of the healing of the Gerasene demoniac (Lk 8:26–39) and the calming of the storm at sea (Lk 8:22–25).

Jairus was probably one of the elders who oversaw the local synagogue. His social status was much greater than that of the woman afflicted with hemorrhages (bleeding), who would have been considered ritually unclean because of her continuous flow of blood, and therefore unfit for contact with others. The parallel account in Mark 5:21–43 says that although she spent all she had seeking a cure, the care she had received from various doctors only caused her great suffering. Do you know anyone in a similar situation?

To help you imagine the interior of Jairus's house, see the description of a typical home in "A Brief Tour of First-Century Palestine."

Consider ...

- Who are you in this story? You could be the woman with the hemorrhage, Jairus or his wife, someone in the crowd along the way, one of the mourners, one of the apostles, or the little girl.
- What do you see, hear, and feel? What is the jostling crowd around Jesus like? Can you imagine the particular features of each of the main characters in this story? How does the inside of Jairus's house feel different from the scene outside on the busy street?

- What do you notice about Jesus? How do your feelings toward him shift as this story unfolds?
- This story has two main parts; consider whether you will focus on the healing of the woman with the flow of blood, the raising of Jairus's daughter, or both.

Walk with Jesus

Take a moment to pray for what your heart most desires from this encounter with Jesus.

Then let the Holy Spirit be your guide as you enter the Gospel story.

As you finish walking with Jesus, share your thoughts, feelings, and desires with God, much as one friend would speak to another.

Reflect on the Journey

After you are finished praying, savor and reflect on your experience, either in your prayer journal or with your prayer group. Begin by writing or sharing the story of your imaginative prayer journey: What happened during your time with Jesus? Then consider the following questions:

- The woman with the flow of blood wants to hide from Jesus, but he persistently seeks her out. How is your own relationship with Jesus like this, if at all?
- "Do not trouble the teacher" (Lk 8:49). Do you ever feel that your situation is too hopeless to bring to Jesus?
- Jesus admonishes the parents of the young girl to keep her raising a secret. Do you tend to keep Jesus' work in your own life a secret from others? Why or why not?

$$\left(15\right)$$

Jesus Sends His Disciples to Proclaim the Kingdom

(Lk 10:1–12, 17–20)

Be with Jesus as he sends his disciples out ahead
of him to proclaim the kingdom of God.

Prepare

Take a few moments to quietly welcome God's presence.

Lord, thank you for meeting me here in prayer. Thank you for loving me. Please give me the grace to love and serve you in all my thoughts, words, and actions.

Jesus, let me be with your disciples as you send them ahead of you to preach the kingdom of God. Let your Spirit breathe in me, enlivening my imagination so that I can grow closer to you. Amen.

Read

LUKE 10:1–12, 17–20

After this the Lord appointed seventy others and sent them on ahead of him in pairs to every town and place where he himself intended to go. He said to them, "The harvest is plentiful, but the laborers are few; therefore ask the Lord of the harvest to send out laborers into his harvest. Go on your way. See, I am sending you out like lambs into the midst of wolves. Carry no purse, no bag, no sandals; and greet no one on the road. Whatever house you enter, first say, 'Peace to this house!' And if anyone is there who shares in peace, your peace will rest on that person; but if not, it will return to you. Remain in the same house, eating and drinking whatever they provide, for the laborer deserves to be paid. Do not move about from house to house. Whenever you enter a town and its people welcome you, eat what is set before you; cure the sick who are there, and say to them, 'The kingdom of God has come near to you.' But whenever you enter a town and they do not welcome you, go out into its streets and say, 'Even the dust of your town that clings to our feet, we wipe off in protest against you. Yet know this: the kingdom of God has come near.' I tell you, on that day it will be more tolerable for Sodom than for that town."

The seventy returned with joy, saying, "Lord, in your name even the demons submit to us!" He said to them, "I watched Satan fall from heaven like a flash of lightning. See, I have given you authority to tread on snakes and scorpions, and over all the power of the enemy; and nothing will hurt you. Nevertheless, do not rejoice at this, that the spirits submit to you, but rejoice that your names are written in heaven."

✠

Set the Scene

This is the second time in the Gospel of Luke that Jesus sends his disciples out ahead of him; the first is in the previous chapter, when he sends the twelve apostles out to proclaim the kingdom of God and heal the sick (Lk 9:1–6). As in that account, Jesus directs the disciples to travel in pairs without relying on their own resources, but on God, one another, and the hospitality of those they meet along the way. Their mission is so urgent that they shouldn't even stop to talk to others they might meet on the road along the way. The disciples are to be emissaries of God's peace, but should at the same time expect that they will not be welcomed everywhere.

Providing hospitality to the traveler was a sacred imperative throughout the ancient Near East, and failing to provide such hospitality was seen as an act of hostility. Hosts and guests followed strict protocols: The host was to personally greet and serve his guests, providing them with water for washing their feet, food and drink, shelter for the night, and protection. Guests, in turn, were to offer a blessing on the household, to accept what was offered, and not to take advantage of their host.

By shaking the dust off their feet as they left an unwelcoming town, the disciples were testifying to the town's failure to provide even basic hospitality.

For background on the difficulties of travel, see "A Brief Tour of First-Century Palestine," where you can also read about a typical house and the requirements of hospitality.

Consider ...

- Who are you in this story? And with whom will you travel? (Remember, the disciples are to go forth in pairs.)
- What do you see, hear, and feel as you set forth on your journey? Whom do you meet along the way? What is the weather like?
- How do you feel about Jesus as this story unfolds?
- Think about what part of this story you will focus on. You might focus on talking to Jesus about his instruc-

tions, walking down the road with your companion, or entering a village to proclaim the good news.

Walk with Jesus

Take a moment to pray for what your heart most desires from this encounter with Jesus.

Then let the Holy Spirit be your guide as you enter the Gospel story.

As you finish walking with Jesus, share your thoughts, feelings, and desires with God, much as one friend would speak to another.

Reflect on the Journey

After you are finished praying, savor and reflect on your experience, either in your prayer journal or with your prayer group. Begin by writing or sharing the story of your imaginative prayer journey: What happened during your time with Jesus? Then consider the following questions:

- What did you make of Jesus' instructions to travel so lightly — without money or even sandals? How does precarity make you feel?
- Have you ever shared the message of Jesus with others? How was that message received?
- What would it be like for you to live out this story in the present day? Do you know anyone who lives like that today?

(16)

Jesus Heals the Bent Woman

(Lk 13:10–17)

Be with Jesus as he heals a woman who has been
unable to stand straight for eighteen years.

Prepare

Take a few moments to quietly welcome God's presence.

Lord, thank you for meeting me here in prayer. Thank you for loving me. Please give me the grace to love and serve you in all my
thoughts, words, and actions.

Jesus, allow me to join you today in the synagogue as you call
the bent woman to stand. Let your Spirit breathe in me, enlivening
my imagination so that I can grow closer to you. Amen.

Read

LUKE 13:10–17

Now he was teaching in one of the synagogues on the sabbath. And just then there appeared a woman with a spirit that had crippled her for eighteen years. She was bent over and was quite unable to stand up straight. When Jesus saw her, he called her over and said, "Woman, you are set free from your ailment." When he laid his hands on her, immediately she stood up straight and began praising God. But the leader of the synagogue, indignant because Jesus had cured on the sabbath, kept saying to the crowd, "There are six days on which work ought to be done; come on those days and be cured, not on the sabbath day." But the Lord answered him and said, "You hypocrites! Does not each of you on the sabbath untie his ox or his donkey from the manger, and lead it away to give it water? And ought not this woman, a daughter of Abraham whom Satan bound for eighteen long years, be set free from this bondage on the sabbath day?" When he said this, all his opponents were put to shame; and the entire crowd was rejoicing at all the wonderful things that he was doing.

✠

Set the Scene

This story begins by noting that Jesus was teaching in the synagogue (see "A Brief Tour of First-Century Palestine" for background on synagogues).

The story turns on the question of whether Jesus ought to be healing the woman on the sabbath. The religious leaders of Jesus' time taught that the law of Moses allowed for healing someone on the sabbath if the person were at risk of dying, but in cases where death wasn't imminent, healing was not allowed.

Note that, unlike most of Jesus' healings, the bent woman does not ask for healing; Jesus simply offers it. As his words indicate, the people of his day considered illness and disability to be the work of

Satan or evil spirits.

Consider ...

- Who are you in this story? The bent woman? A member of the congregation? One of the religious leaders?
- Look around: Who else is with you in the synagogue? What does it look and smell like? Where does the light come from?
- What do you notice about Jesus in this story? How do you feel toward him?

Walk with Jesus

Take a moment to pray for what your heart most desires from this encounter with Jesus.

Then let the Holy Spirit be your guide as you enter the Gospel story.

As you finish walking with Jesus, share your thoughts, feelings, and desires with God, much as one friend would speak to another.

Reflect on the Journey

After you are finished praying, savor and reflect on your experience, either in your prayer journal or with your prayer group. Begin by writing or sharing the story of your imaginative prayer journey: What happened during your time with Jesus? Then consider the following questions:

- The woman doesn't ask Jesus for healing; he just singles her out and tells her that she is free. How would it feel for Jesus to speak these words to you?
- Do you ever feel yourself "bent and bound"?
- Do you ever feel Jesus admonishing you for hypocrisy or for placing limits on God?

(17)

The Samaritan Woman at the Well

(Jn 4:4–30, 39–42)

Rest with Jesus at Jacob's well as he encounters a
Samaritan woman who has come to draw water.

Prepare

Take a few moments to quietly welcome God's presence.

Lord, thank you for meeting me here in prayer. Thank you for loving me. Please give me the grace to love and serve you in all my thoughts, words, and actions.

Jesus, allow me to join you by Jacob's well as you offer rest, and life, to the Samaritan woman. Let your Spirit breathe in me, enlivening my imagination so that I can grow closer to you. Amen.

Read

JOHN 4:4–30, 39–42

But he had to go through Samaria. So he came to a Samaritan city called Sychar, near the plot of ground that Jacob had given to his son Joseph. Jacob's well was there, and Jesus, tired out by his journey, was sitting by the well. It was about noon.

A Samaritan woman came to draw water, and Jesus said to her, "Give me a drink." (His disciples had gone to the city to buy food.) The Samaritan woman said to him, "How is it that you, a Jew, ask a drink of me, a woman of Samaria?" (Jews do not share things in common with Samaritans.) Jesus answered her, "If you knew the gift of God, and who it is that is saying to you, 'Give me a drink,' you would have asked him, and he would have given you living water." The woman said to him, "Sir, you have no bucket, and the well is deep. Where do you get that living water? Are you greater than our ancestor Jacob, who gave us the well, and with his sons and his flocks drank from it?" Jesus said to her, "Everyone who drinks of this water will be thirsty again, but those who drink of the water that I will give them will never be thirsty. The water that I will give will become in them a spring of water gushing up to eternal life." The woman said to him, "Sir, give me this water, so that I may never be thirsty or have to keep coming here to draw water."

Jesus said to her, "Go, call your husband, and come back." The woman answered him, "I have no husband." Jesus said to her, "You are right in saying, 'I have no husband'; for you have had five husbands, and the one you have now is not your husband. What you have said is true!" The woman said to him, "Sir, I see that you are a prophet. Our ancestors worshiped on this mountain, but you say that the place where people must worship is in Jerusalem." Jesus said to her, "Woman, believe me, the hour is coming when you will worship the Father neither on this mountain nor in Jerusalem. You worship what you do not know; we worship what we know, for salvation is from the Jews. But the hour is coming, and is now here, when the true worshipers will worship the Father in spirit and truth, for the Father seeks such as these to worship him. God is spirit, and those who worship him must worship in spirit and truth." The woman said to him, "I know that the Messiah is coming" (who is called Christ). "When he comes, he will proclaim all things to us." Jesus said to her, "I am he, the one who is speaking to you."

Just then his disciples came. They were astonished that he was speaking with a woman, but no one said, "What do you want?" or, "Why are you speaking with her?" Then the woman left her water jar and went back to the city. She said to the people, "Come and see a man who told me everything I have ever done! He cannot be the Messiah, can he?" They left the city and were on their way to him.

Many Samaritans from that city believed in him because of the woman's testimony, "He told me everything I have ever done." So when the Samaritans came to him, they asked him to stay with them; and he stayed there two days. And many more believed because of his word. They said to the woman, "It is no longer because of what you said that we believe, for we have heard for ourselves, and we know that this is truly the Savior of the world."

✠

Set the Scene

Jesus and his disciples are passing through Samaria on their way back to Galilee after spending time in Judea; the journey would have taken about three days (see "A Brief Tour of First-Century Palestine" for more information about Samaria and Samaritans).

Some of the conversation between Jesus and the Samaritan woman plays on the tension between Samaritans and Jews. For example, Samaritans and Jews disagreed about the location God designated for the Temple; Samaritans regarded Mount Gerizim as the proper site for temple worship, while Jews worshiped at the Temple in Jerusalem.

Jesus stops to rest at Jacob's well, a large well (about seven feet around and more than one hundred feet deep) about half a mile from the Samaritan town of Sychar, also known as Shechem. The well is traditionally believed to sit on the plot of land that Jacob purchased (Gn 33:18–20) and is located near a mountain pass. The area is dry and rocky and rich in its associations with Abraham and Old Testament history.

Consider ...

- Who are you in this story? You might choose to imagine the story as the Samaritan woman. Or maybe you are a silent, invisible observer, one of the disciples as they return to find Jesus speaking with the woman, or one of the local residents.
- Imagine the well, far from the town and surrounded by dry land. What do you see, hear, and smell? What does the path to the well look like? Can you see the Samaritan town in the distance?
- How does Jesus' expression and tone of voice change over the course of the conversation?
- Besides focusing on the exchange Jesus has with the woman, another option would be to imagine Jesus and his disciples during the two days they spend in the Samaritan town.

Walk with Jesus

Take a moment to pray for what your heart most desires from this encounter with Jesus.

Then let the Holy Spirit be your guide as you enter the Gospel story.

As you finish walking with Jesus, share your thoughts, feelings, and desires with God, much as one friend would speak to another.

Reflect on the Journey

After you are finished praying, savor and reflect on your experience, either in your prayer journal or with your prayer group. Begin by writing or sharing the story of your imaginative prayer journey: What happened during your time with Jesus? Then consider the following questions:

- The Samaritan woman is wary and skeptical of Jesus. Have you ever felt the same way?
- The Samaritan woman does not hesitate to engage Jesus in lively banter, questioning and even challenging him. What is your own conversation with Jesus like?
- The woman is reluctant to divulge her story to Jesus, but in the end, she tells her neighbors, "He told me everything I have ever done" (Jn 4:39). What part of your own story do you hide from Jesus?

(18)

Jesus Feeds the People

(Mt 14:14–20)

Be with Jesus as he helps the disciples feed the great
crowds of people who have come to be healed by him.

Prepare

Take a few moments to quietly welcome God's presence.

Lord, thank you for meeting me here in prayer. Thank you for loving me. Please give me the grace to love and serve you in all my
thoughts, words, and actions.

Jesus, allow me to join you as you heal and feed the multitudes.
Let your Spirit breathe in me, enlivening my imagination so that I
can grow closer to you. Amen.

Read

MATTHEW 14:14–20

When he went ashore, he saw a great crowd; and he had compassion for them and cured their sick. When it was evening, the disciples came to him and said, "This is a deserted place, and the hour is now late; send the crowds away so that they may go into the villages and buy food for themselves." Jesus said to them, "They need not go away; you give them something to eat." They replied, "We have nothing here but five loaves and two fish." And he said, "Bring them here to me." Then he ordered the crowds to sit down on the grass. Taking the five loaves and the two fish, he looked up to heaven, and blessed and broke the loaves, and gave them to the disciples, and the disciples gave them to the crowds. And all ate and were filled; and they took up what was left over of the broken pieces, twelve baskets full.

✠

Set the Scene

This story comes on the heels of the death of John the Baptist. In Matthew's telling of this miracle story, Jesus withdraws to a deserted place after learning of the death of John. The crowds follow him there (Mt 14:3–13).

Jews of Jesus' time would have seen this miracle as echoing the miraculous feeding of the Israelites in the desert; the coming messiah was expected to repeat this miracle.

This is the only one of Jesus' miracles that is mentioned in all four Gospels. In the parallel story in John 6:5–13, the five loaves and two fish are supplied by a boy — a detail you may wish to work into your prayer.

Consider ...

- Who are you in this story? One of the disciples? Someone in the crowd?

- Can you imagine this vast crowd gathered by the seashore? What do you see, hear, and smell? Can you pick out a few individuals? How do you feel?
- What do you notice about Jesus? What is he doing as the people eat their food?

Walk with Jesus

Take a moment to pray for what your heart most desires from this encounter with Jesus.

Then let the Holy Spirit be your guide as you enter the Gospel story.

As you finish walking with Jesus, share your thoughts, feelings, and desires with God, much as one friend would speak to another.

Reflect on the Journey

After you are finished praying, savor and reflect on your experience, either in your prayer journal or with your prayer group. Begin by writing or sharing the story of your imaginative prayer journey: What happened during your time with Jesus? Then consider the following questions:

- If Jesus were to ask you to feed the "crowds" in your own life, what would your "five loaves and two fish" be?
- What are you hungry for? How does Jesus feed you?
- Have you ever witnessed unexpected abundance coming out of scarcity? Where was God in that experience?

(19)

Jesus Calls Peter to Walk on Water

(Mt 14:22–33)

Walk with Jesus across a stormy sea toward his
disciples, including the impetuous Peter.

Prepare

Take a few moments to quietly welcome God's presence.

Lord, thank you for meeting me here in prayer. Thank you for loving me. Please give me the grace to love and serve you in all my
thoughts, words, and actions.

Jesus, let me be with you as you call Peter to get out of the boat
in order to meet you in the storm. Let your Spirit breathe in me,
enlivening my imagination so that I can grow closer to you. Amen.

Read

MATTHEW 14:22–33

Immediately he made the disciples get into the boat and go on ahead to the other side, while he dismissed the crowds. And after he had dismissed the crowds, he went up the mountain by himself to pray. When evening came, he was there alone, but by this time the boat, battered by the waves, was far from the land, for the wind was against them. And early in the morning he came walking toward them on the sea. But when the disciples saw him walking on the sea, they were terrified, saying, "It is a ghost!" And they cried out in fear. But immediately Jesus spoke to them and said, "Take heart, it is I; do not be afraid."

Peter answered him, "Lord, if it is you, command me to come to you on the water." He said, "Come." So Peter got out of the boat, started walking on the water, and came toward Jesus. But when he noticed the strong wind, he became frightened, and beginning to sink, he cried out, "Lord, save me!" Jesus immediately reached out his hand and caught him, saying to him, "You of little faith, why did you doubt?" When they got into the boat, the wind ceased. And those in the boat worshiped him, saying, "Truly you are the Son of God."

✠

Set the Scene

This story follows immediately after Jesus feeds the crowds by multiplying the loaves and fish (reading guide #18). It opens with Jesus dismissing the crowds and once again withdrawing to pray by himself, this time on a mountain-top; recall that he had recently learned of the death of John the Baptist.

As noted above in reading guide #12, "Jesus Calms the Stormy Sea," the Sea of Galilee can see waves of six feet or more in a windstorm. Moreover, although Peter and some of Jesus' other disciples were fishermen and expert boatmen, they probably could not swim. See "A Brief Tour of First-Century Palestine" for more about the Sea of Galilee.

The time would have been between 3:00 a.m. and 6:00 a.m.

Consider ...

- Who are you in this story? Peter or one of the other people in the boat?
- Imagine yourself in the boat after having spent hours fighting against the wind. What do you see, feel, and hear during the storm? What is the mood in the boat before Jesus shows up?
- What does Jesus look like as he approaches the boat? What about his face?

Walk with Jesus

Take a moment to pray for what your heart most desires from this encounter with Jesus.

Then let the Holy Spirit be your guide as you enter the Gospel story.

As you finish walking with Jesus, share your thoughts, feelings, and desires with God, much as one friend would speak to another.

Reflect on the Journey

After you are finished praying, savor and reflect on your experience, either in your prayer journal or with your prayer group. Begin by writing or sharing the story of your imaginative prayer journey: What happened during your time with Jesus? Then consider the following questions:

- In the stormy night, the disciples don't recognize Jesus; Peter seems to require further proof, even after Jesus identifies himself. Do you ever doubt Jesus' presence in the storms of your own life?

- Peter is willing to take a big risk in order to get to Jesus. What would "getting out of the boat" look like for you?
- Have you ever cried out, "Lord, save me!" What happened?

(20)

Jesus Heals a Blind Man

(Mk 10:46–52)

Walk with Jesus along the road to Jericho, as he
encounters a blind beggar calling his name.

Prepare

Take a few moments to quietly welcome God's presence.

Lord, thank you for meeting me here in prayer. Thank you for loving me. Please give me the grace to love and serve you in all my thoughts, words, and actions.

Jesus, let me be with you as you ask the blind man what he wants. Let your Spirit breathe in me, enlivening my imagination so that I can grow closer to you. Amen.

Read

MARK 10:46–52

They came to Jericho. As he and his disciples and a large crowd were leaving Jericho, Bartimaeus son of Timaeus, a blind beggar, was sitting by the roadside. When he heard that it was Jesus of Nazareth, he began to shout out and say, "Jesus, son of David, have mercy on me!" Many sternly ordered him to be quiet, but he cried out even more loudly, "Son of David, have mercy on me!" Jesus stood still and said, "Call him here." And they called the blind man, saying to him, "Take heart; get up, he is calling you." So throwing off his cloak, he sprang up and came to Jesus. Then Jesus said to him, "What do you want me to do for you?" The blind man said to him, "My teacher, let me see again." Jesus said to him, "Go; your faith has made you well." Immediately he regained his sight and followed him on the way.

☩

Set the Scene

Jesus encounters Bartimaeus as he approaches the city of Jericho, which sits on a plain about fifteen miles northeast of Jerusalem. Abundant natural fountains and streams support agricultural cultivation, including groves of fruit trees, especially palms. King Herod the Great built a palace, a theater, and other fine buildings in Jericho, making it a retreat for the wealthy aristocracy.

This story immediately follows another story in the Gospel of Mark in which Jesus also invites two of his apostles, James and John, to tell him what he can do for them (Mk 10:35–37) — although in their case, they don't quite get what they asked for.

Consider ...

- Who are you in this story? The blind man, a disciple of Jesus, someone in the crowd, the one who brings the blind man to Jesus, or someone else?

- Imagine the scene alongside the road outside Jericho. What do you hear, smell, and feel? Is the city nearby? What do you notice about the different voices in this story?
- What do you notice about Jesus? How do you think Bartimaeus would have experienced his presence without being able to see him?

Walk with Jesus

Take a moment to pray for what your heart most desires from this encounter with Jesus.

Then let the Holy Spirit be your guide as you enter the Gospel story.

As you finish walking with Jesus, share your thoughts, feelings, and desires with God, much as one friend would speak to another.

Reflect on the Journey

After you are finished praying, savor and reflect on your experience, either in your prayer journal or with your prayer group. Begin by writing or sharing the story of your imaginative prayer journey: What happened during your time with Jesus? Then consider the following questions:

- This story is full of many competing voices: those of Bartimaeus, the crowd, Jesus, and the one who encourages Bartimaeus and leads him to Jesus. Which voices dominate your own life with Jesus?
- Jesus now asks you, "What do you want me to do for you?" Your answer?
- What might you lose or give up if Jesus grants your request?

(21)

The Transfiguration
of Jesus

(Mt 17:1–8)

Climb a mountain with Jesus, where his glory
will be revealed to Peter, James, and John.

Prepare

Take a few moments to quietly welcome God's presence.

Lord, thank you for meeting me here in prayer. Thank you for loving me. Please give me the grace to love and serve you in all my thoughts, words, and actions.

Jesus, let me be with you on the mountaintop as your glory is revealed to your friends. Let your Spirit breathe in me, enlivening my imagination so that I can grow closer to you. Amen.

Read

MATTHEW 17:1–8

Six days later, Jesus took with him Peter and James and his brother John and led them up a high mountain, by themselves. And he was transfigured before them, and his face shone like the sun, and his clothes became dazzling white. Suddenly there appeared to them Moses and Elijah, talking with him. Then Peter said to Jesus, "Lord, it is good for us to be here; if you wish, I will make three dwellings here, one for you, one for Moses, and one for Elijah." While he was still speaking, suddenly a bright cloud overshadowed them, and from the cloud a voice said, "This is my Son, the Beloved; with him I am well pleased; listen to him!" When the disciples heard this, they fell to the ground and were overcome by fear. But Jesus came and touched them, saying, "Get up and do not be afraid." And when they looked up, they saw no one except Jesus himself alone.

✠

Set the Scene

Jesus takes Peter, James, and John up a mountain to pray. The location of the Transfiguration has traditionally been associated with Mount Tabor (elevation: 636 feet), or Mount Hermon (9,232 feet); some Scripture scholars suggest Mount Carmel (1,724 feet) as a possible site. Whatever the actual location, ascending the mountain would have involved more than a casual hike. The Gospel may simply want readers to recall how Moses met God on Mount Sinai (Ex 24:16).

The entire story is laced with references to the Old Testament. A few of these are especially helpful to know for imaginative prayer. Moses and Elijah are the two most important figures of the Old Testament: Moses represents the Law, while Elijah represents the tradition of wonder-working prophets. Also, Peter's strange suggestion about building three dwellings (or tents) is a reference to the Jewish festival of Sukkot, or the Feast of Shelters or Booths — a seven-day harvest festival during which Jews were required to make a pilgrimage to Jerusalem.

Consider ...

- Who are you in this story? One of the three disciples or another observer?
- What do you see, feel, and hear on the journey up the mountainside? What do the men take along with them? What is the top of the mountain like, and what can you see from that height?
- What does the transfigured Jesus look like? How do you feel toward him?

Walk with Jesus

Take a moment to pray for what your heart most desires from this encounter with Jesus.

Then let the Holy Spirit be your guide as you enter the Gospel story.

As you finish walking with Jesus, share your thoughts, feelings, and desires with God, much as one friend would speak to another.

Reflect on the Journey

After you are finished praying, savor and reflect on your experience, either in your prayer journal or with your prayer group. Begin by writing or sharing the story of your imaginative prayer journey: What happened during your time with Jesus? Then consider the following questions:

- Have you ever experienced a "transfiguration," a peak experience that changed you? If so, where was God in that?
- How do you feel about the glorified Jesus? Can you identify with the disciples' reactions to their experi-

ence of the Transfiguration?

- How was your journey down the mountain with Jesus and the other disciples different from the journey up? What questions did you want to ask Jesus?

(22)

The Woman Caught in Adultery

(Jn 8:2–11)

Follow Jesus to the Temple, where the scribes and Pharisees present him with a woman caught in the act of adultery, asking him to judge her according to the law of Moses.

Prepare

Take a few moments to quietly welcome God's presence.

Lord, thank you for meeting me here in prayer. Thank you for loving me. Please give me the grace to love and serve you in all my thoughts, words, and actions.

Jesus, let me stand with you as you teach about judgment and mercy. Let your Spirit breathe in me, enlivening my imagination so

that I can grow closer to you. Amen.

Read

JOHN 8:2–11

Early in the morning he came again to the temple. All the people came to him and he sat down and began to teach them. The scribes and the Pharisees brought a woman who had been caught in adultery; and making her stand before all of them, they said to him, "Teacher, this woman was caught in the very act of committing adultery. Now in the law Moses commanded us to stone such women. Now what do you say?" They said this to test him, so that they might have some charge to bring against him. Jesus bent down and wrote with his finger on the ground. When they kept on questioning him, he straightened up and said to them, "Let anyone among you who is without sin be the first to throw a stone at her." And once again he bent down and wrote on the ground. When they heard it, they went away, one by one, beginning with the elders; and Jesus was left alone with the woman standing before him. Jesus straightened up and said to her, "Woman, where are they? Has no one condemned you?" She said, "No one, sir." And Jesus said, "Neither do I condemn you. Go your way, and from now on do not sin again."

✠

Set the Scene

This episode occurs in the Temple area during Sukkot, a harvest festival that would have drawn pilgrims to Jerusalem. Jesus has been teaching in the Temple area for several days and increasingly clashing with the religious authorities. See "A Brief Tour of First-Century Palestine" for more about Jerusalem and the Temple.

The law prescribed that both parties caught in the act of adultery (the man and the woman) be put to death (Lv 20:10), with the first stones being thrown by the witnesses who testified against them.

What did Jesus write in the dust? Some early commentators supposed Jesus was writing the sins of the woman's accusers in the dust, but no one really knows; it might be that the author of the Gospel wants us to come up with our own ideas.

Consider ...

- Who are you in this story? Someone in the crowd? One of the woman's accusers? Or the accused?
- What do you see, hear, and smell here in the precincts of the Temple? Remember that this story occurs during a harvest festival and Jerusalem would be crowded with pilgrims.
- What do you imagine Jesus writing in the dust?

Walk with Jesus

Take a moment to pray for what your heart most desires from this encounter with Jesus.

Then let the Holy Spirit be your guide as you enter the Gospel story.

As you finish walking with Jesus, share your thoughts, feelings, and desires with God, much as one friend would speak to another.

Reflect on the Journey

After you are finished praying, savor and reflect on your experience, either in your prayer journal or with your prayer group. Begin by writing or sharing the story of your imaginative prayer journey: What happened during your time with Jesus? Then consider the following questions:

- What are the stones in your hands? Have you ever been part of a group that accused someone?
- Have you ever been tempted to test Jesus?

- Have you ever felt like the accused woman? What do you hear Jesus saying to you about that?

(23)

Martha and Mary

(Lk 10:38–42)

Walk with Jesus as he is welcomed into the
home of his friends Martha and Mary.

Prepare
Take a few moments to quietly welcome God's presence.

Lord, thank you for meeting me here in prayer. Thank you for loving me. Please give me the grace to love and serve you in all my thoughts, words, and actions.

Jesus, let me rest with you in the home of Mary and Martha. Let your Spirit breathe in me, enlivening my imagination so that I can grow closer to you. Amen.

Read

Now as they went on their way, he entered a certain village, where a woman named Martha welcomed him into her home. She had a sister named Mary, who sat at the Lord's feet and listened to what he was saying. But Martha was distracted by her many tasks; so she came to him and asked, "Lord, do you not care that my sister has left me to do all the work by myself? Tell her then to help me." But the Lord answered her, "Martha, Martha, you are worried and distracted by many things; there is need of only one thing. Mary has chosen the better part, which will not be taken away from her."

☧

Set the Scene

Jesus has just recently sent seventy of his disciples ahead of him to proclaim the kingdom of God in every place he intended to visit; after their return, he tells the parable of the Good Samaritan.

Then Jesus and his disciples travel to Bethany, where a woman named Martha welcomes him into the home she shares with her sister, Mary, and her brother, Lazarus. Bethany was a village located about two miles from Jerusalem. Jesus often stayed in Bethany when he visited Jerusalem, perhaps in the home of his friends.

See "A Brief Tour of First-Century Palestine" to help you imagine what a typical home would have looked like. Cooking would probably have occurred in an outdoor kitchen in the courtyard. Food was typically cooked over an open fire in cauldrons or clay pots, fried on a heated stone or a bed of hot coals on the ground, or baked in a makeshift stone or clay oven.

Mary's position, sitting at the feet of Jesus, was the posture of a disciple. While it was not unheard of for women in Israel to receive (and give) instruction in synagogues and homes, neither was it typical. Only boys attended Torah school, for example.

Consider ...

- Who are you in this story? Mary? Martha? One of the disciples?
- Imagine being in Martha's house. Is it big or small? Dim or well lit? Messy or neat? What do you see lying around? What does the cooking food smell like?
- What do you notice about the way Jesus speaks to Mary? How about Martha?

Walk with Jesus

Take a moment to pray for what your heart most desires from this encounter with Jesus.

Then let the Holy Spirit be your guide as you enter the Gospel story.

As you finish walking with Jesus, share your thoughts, feelings, and desires with God, much as one friend would speak to another.

Reflect on the Journey

After you are finished praying, savor and reflect on your experience, either in your prayer journal or with your prayer group. Begin by writing or sharing the story of your imaginative prayer journey: What happened during your time with Jesus? Then consider the following questions:

- Are you more of a "Mary" or a "Martha"? What are you most anxious and worried about?
- What do you think happened after Jesus' reply to Martha? What would you have done in Martha's place?
- How do you welcome Jesus into your own home?

(24)

Jesus and the Little Children

(Mt 18:1–5; 19:13–15)

Walk with Jesus as he welcomes children, pointing
to them as emblems of the kingdom of God.

Prepare

Take a few moments to quietly welcome God's presence.

Lord, thank you for meeting me here in prayer. Thank you for loving me. Please give me the grace to love and serve you in all my
thoughts, words, and actions.

Jesus, let me join you as you bless the children. Let your Spirit
breathe in me, enlivening my imagination so that I can grow closer
to you. Amen.

Read

MATTHEW 18:1–5; 19:13–15

At that time the disciples came to Jesus and asked, "Who is the greatest in the kingdom of heaven?" He called a child, whom he put among them, and said, "Truly I tell you, unless you change and become like children, you will never enter the kingdom of heaven. Whoever becomes humble like this child is the greatest in the kingdom of heaven. Whoever welcomes one such child in my name welcomes me."

Then little children were being brought to him in order that he might lay his hands on them and pray. The disciples spoke sternly to those who brought them; but Jesus said, "Let the little children come to me, and do not stop them; for it is to such as these that the kingdom of heaven belongs." And he laid his hands on them and went on his way.

✠

Set the Scene

The first part of this story takes place in Capernaum; the second, somewhere in Judea. Even though they are separate accounts, for the purpose of your prayer, you may wish to treat them as one episode.

Children were much desired and valued in ancient Israel. They were nursed for two to three years. Infants were swaddled and carried around in baskets strapped to their mother's backs, and toddlers were carried in slings or portable hammocks that could be hung up on a hook to keep a child from wandering off.

Children shared in the work of their parents from an early age, helping with household chores or in the fields. Parents took the lead role in teaching children religious precepts and basic literacy in the home. Older boys would go on to attend school in the local synagogue, with the Scriptures being their only textbook.

Children also had time for play, and archaeologists have found various toys, including spinning disks, child-sized clay vessels (some made by adults, others apparently made by children), and rattles. These toys have often been found concentrated in one part of the house, leading scholars to speculate that children may have had a designated area within the home for playing and keeping toys.

Consider ...

- Who are you in this story? A child? A disciple? Someone else, such as a mother?
- Imagine the setting for this story. Where are you? What do you see and hear? How many children are there? Think of the child Jesus calls to him — the one he uses to illustrate the kingdom of heaven. What is this child like, and how does he or she react?
- What do you notice about Jesus? How does he interact with each child?

Walk with Jesus

Take a moment to pray for what your heart most desires from this encounter with Jesus.

Then let the Holy Spirit be your guide as you enter the Gospel story.

As you finish walking with Jesus, share your thoughts, feelings, and desires with God, much as one friend would speak to another.

Reflect on the Journey

After you are finished praying, savor and reflect on your experience, either in your prayer journal or with your prayer group. Begin by writing or sharing the story of your imaginative prayer journey: What happened during your time with Jesus? Then consider the following questions:

- How did you relate to Jesus when you were a child?
- Jesus says that to enter the kingdom of heaven, we must become like children. Can you find such a child in yourself? What would need to change for you to become like a child again?
- Imagine yourself as a child. How does this childlike perspective change the way you approach Jesus?

(25)

Jesus Invites Himself to Zacchaeus's House

(Lk 19:2–10)

Walk with Jesus as he invites himself to the home of Zacchaeus, one of the chief tax collectors.

Prepare

Take a few moments to quietly welcome God's presence.

Lord, thank you for meeting me here in prayer. Thank you for loving me. Please give me the grace to love and serve you in all my thoughts, words, and actions.

Jesus, allow me to walk with you as you invite yourself to the home of Zacchaeus. Let your Spirit breathe in me, enlivening my imagination so that I can grow closer to you. Amen.

Read

LUKE 19:2–10

A man was there named Zacchaeus; he was a chief tax collector and was rich. He was trying to see who Jesus was, but on account of the crowd he could not, because he was short in stature. So he ran ahead and climbed a sycamore tree to see him, because he was going to pass that way. When Jesus came to the place, he looked up and said to him, "Zacchaeus, hurry and come down; for I must stay at your house today." So he hurried down and was happy to welcome him. All who saw it began to grumble and said, "He has gone to be the guest of one who is a sinner." Zacchaeus stood there and said to the Lord, "Look, half of my possessions, Lord, I will give to the poor; and if I have defrauded anyone of anything, I will pay back four times as much." Then Jesus said to him, "Today salvation has come to this house, because he too is a son of Abraham. For the Son of Man came to seek out and to save the lost."

✠

Set the Scene

Jesus is entering Jericho as this story opens. As mentioned earlier ("Jesus Heals a Blind Man," reading guide #20), Jericho sits on a plain about fifteen miles northeast of Jerusalem. The area was fertile and well watered, supporting extensive agriculture, including many groves of fruit trees. It was also a retreat for the wealthy aristocracy; King Herod the Great built his winter palace there, along with a theater and other fine buildings.

The sycamore is a large fig-bearing tree with a wide, dense, dark-green crown, papery bark with a yellowish or orangish tint, and fruit that ripens from bright green to yellow or red. Assuming the tree was mature, its branches could have easily extended over the road.

As also mentioned earlier ("Jesus Calls Matthew and Eats with Sinners," reading guide #13), tax collectors were among the most despised members of Israelite society, considered thieves and traitors for collaborating with the occupying Roman forces. They were also relatively wealthy, so Zacchaeus's home would have been more luxurious than most; see "A Brief Tour of First-Century Palestine" for details about what such a home would have been like.

Consider ...

- Who are you in this story? Are you Zacchaeus? A follower of Jesus? Perhaps a fellow tax collector? Maybe just an onlooker?
- What do you see and hear during this story? What does the sycamore tree smell like? If you go with Jesus to Zacchaeus's house, what do you see, hear, smell, and taste there?
- What do you notice about Jesus? What is his tone of voice like as he speaks to Zacchaeus?

Walk with Jesus

Take a moment to pray for what your heart most desires from this encounter with Jesus.

Then let the Holy Spirit be your guide as you enter the Gospel story.

As you finish walking with Jesus, share your thoughts, feelings, and desires with God, much as one friend would speak to another.

Reflect on the Journey

After you are finished praying, savor and reflect on your experience, either in your prayer journal or with your prayer group. Begin by writing or sharing the story of your imaginative prayer journey: What happened during your time with Jesus? Then consider the following questions:

- Zacchaeus climbed a sycamore tree to get a better view

of Jesus. What do you do to get a better view of Jesus?

- How would you respond if Jesus said he wanted to dine at your house tonight? Would you feel ready to receive him as a guest?
- Zacchaeus offers to give up half his possessions as well as the practice of extortion. What have you given up to welcome Jesus into your life?

(26)

The Raising of Lazarus

(Jn 11:1–7, 17–44)

Walk with Jesus as he travels back to Bethany at the request
of Mary and Martha, whose brother, Lazarus, has died.

Prepare

Take a few moments to quietly welcome God's presence.

Lord, thank you for meeting me here in prayer. Thank you for loving me. Please give me the grace to love and serve you in all my
thoughts, words, and actions.

Jesus, let me stand alongside you as you raise Lazarus from the
dead. Let your Spirit breathe in me, enlivening my imagination so
that I can grow closer to you. Amen.

Read

JOHN 11:1–7, 17–44

Now a certain man was ill, Lazarus of Bethany, the village of Mary and her sister Martha. Mary was the one who anointed the Lord with perfume and wiped his feet with her hair; her brother Lazarus was ill. So the sisters sent a message to Jesus, "Lord, he whom you love is ill." But when Jesus heard it, he said, "This illness does not lead to death; rather it is for God's glory, so that the Son of God may be glorified through it." Accordingly, though Jesus loved Martha and her sister and Lazarus, after having heard that Lazarus was ill, he stayed two days longer in the place where he was.

Then after this he said to his disciples, "Let us go to Judea again."

When Jesus arrived, he found that Lazarus had already been in the tomb four days. Now Bethany was near Jerusalem, some two miles away, and many of the Jews had come to Martha and Mary to console them about their brother. When Martha heard that Jesus was coming, she went and met him, while Mary stayed at home. Martha said to Jesus, "Lord, if you had been here, my brother would not have died. But even now I know that God will give you whatever you ask of him." Jesus said to her, "Your brother will rise again." Martha said to him, "I know he will rise again in the resurrection on the last day." Jesus said to her, "I am the resurrection and the life. Those who believe in me, even though they die, will live, and everyone who lives and believes in me will never die. Do you believe this?" She said to him, "Yes, Lord, I believe that you are the Messiah, the Son of God, the one coming into the world."

When she had said this, she went back and called her sister Mary, and told her privately, "The Teacher is here and is calling for you." And when she heard it, she got up quickly and went to him. Now Jesus had not yet come to the village, but was still at the place where Martha had met him. The Jews who were with her in the house, consoling her, saw Mary get up quickly and go out. They followed her because they thought that she was going to the tomb to weep there. When Mary came where Jesus was and saw him, she knelt at his feet and said to him, "Lord, if you had been here, my brother would not have died." When Jesus saw her weeping, and the Jews who came with her also weeping, he was greatly disturbed in spirit and deeply moved. He said, "Where have you laid him?" They said to him, "Lord, come and see." Jesus began to weep. So the Jews said, "See how he loved him!" But some of them said, "Could not he who opened the eyes of the blind man have kept this man from dying?"

Then Jesus, again greatly disturbed, came to the tomb. It was a cave, and a stone was lying against it. Jesus said, "Take away the stone." Martha, the sister of the dead man, said to him, "Lord, already there is a stench because he has been dead four days." Jesus said to her, "Did I not tell you that if you believed, you would see the glory of God?" So they took away the stone. And Jesus looked upward and said, "Father, I thank you for having heard me. I knew that you always hear me, but I have said this for the sake of the crowd standing here, so that they may believe that you sent me." When he had said this, he cried with a loud voice, "Lazarus, come out!" The dead man came out, his hands and feet bound with strips of cloth, and his face wrapped in a cloth. Jesus said to them, "Unbind him, and let him go."

✠

Set the Scene

Like many of the miracle stories in the Gospel of John, the story of the raising of Lazarus is rich with symbolism, foreshadowing, and allusion. For the purpose of this prayer experience, try to focus simply on being present in the narrative.

Mary, Martha, and Lazarus were friends of Jesus with whom he stayed in Bethany when he was visiting Jerusalem. Bethany was just a short distance — about two miles — from Jerusalem.

Jesus receives the sisters' urgent message while he is at the Jordan River, near where John first baptized (Jn 10:40). It is a journey of at least two days from there to Bethany.

In the Gospel of John, this story is the culmination of Jesus' ongoing conflict with the Jewish religious leaders; according to John, this event is the last straw that sets in motion the events that lead to Jesus' death.

Consider ...

- Who are you in this story? You could be one of the sisters, one of their friends, a disciple, or perhaps even Lazarus himself.
- Imagine Martha and Mary's house and imagine the setting of Lazarus's tomb. What do you see, hear, and smell?
- This story is full of emotion: sadness, grief, anger, annoyance, and love. Allow yourself to fully experience the full range of emotions that Jesus and his friends experience.
- What do you notice about Jesus as he weeps for Lazarus?

Walk with Jesus

Take a moment to pray for what your heart most desires from this encounter with Jesus.

Then let the Holy Spirit be your guide as you enter the Gospel story.

As you finish walking with Jesus, share your thoughts, feelings, and desires with God, much as one friend would speak to another.

Reflect on the Journey

After you are finished praying, savor and reflect on your experience, either in your prayer journal or with your prayer group. Begin by writing or sharing the story of your imaginative prayer journey: What happened during your time with Jesus? Then consider the following questions:

- Has Jesus ever wept over you? Has he ever wept with you?
- "Lord, if you had been here, my brother would not have died" (Jn 11:21). Have you ever felt let down by Jesus?
- "Everyone who lives and believes in me will never die. Do you believe this?" (Jn 11:26). How would you answer Jesus' question if you were in Martha's place? What do you imagine your resurrected life will be like?

(27)

Jesus Enters Jerusalem

(Lk 19:35–44)

Walk with Jesus as he enters Jerusalem on the colt
of a donkey, accompanied by a joyful crowd of
disciples who proclaim him the Messiah.

Prepare

Take a few moments to quietly welcome God's presence.

Lord, thank you for meeting me here in prayer. Thank you for loving me. Please give me the grace to love and serve you in all my thoughts, words, and actions.

Jesus, may I walk alongside you as you enter Jerusalem — not triumphantly but humbly. Let your Spirit breathe in me, enlivening my imagination so that I can grow closer to you. Amen.

Read

LUKE 19:35–44

Then they brought it to Jesus; and after throwing their cloaks on the colt, they set Jesus on it. As he rode along, people kept spreading their cloaks on the road. As he was now approaching the path down from the Mount of Olives, the whole multitude of the disciples began to praise God joyfully with a loud voice for all the deeds of power that they had seen, saying,

"Blessed is the king
    who comes in the name of the Lord!
Peace in heaven,
    and glory in the highest heaven!"

Some of the Pharisees in the crowd said to him, "Teacher, order your disciples to stop." He answered, "I tell you, if these were silent, the stones would shout out."

As he came near and saw the city, he wept over it, saying, "If you, even you, had only recognized on this day the things that make for peace! But now they are hidden from your eyes. Indeed, the days will come upon you, when your enemies will set up ramparts around you and surround you, and hem you in on every side. They will crush you to the ground, you and your children within you, and they will not leave within you one stone upon another; because you did not recognize the time of your visitation from God."

✠

Set the Scene

This story follows the story of Jesus' encounter with Zacchaeus in Luke's Gospel. After leaving Jericho, he goes up to Jerusalem (a name that means "city of peace"); as he nears the Mount of Olives, he sends two of his disciples into the village of Bethphage to retrieve a colt (Lk 19:30).

Jesus' choice to enter Jerusalem riding a colt (rather than a war horse) would have been understood by his disciples as a fulfillment of the words of the prophet Zechariah:

> Rejoice greatly, O daughter Zion!
> Shout aloud, O daughter Jerusalem!
> Lo, your king comes to you;
> triumphant and victorious is he,
> humble and riding on a donkey,
> on a colt, the foal of a donkey. (Zechariah 9:9)

The disciples' shouts reflect this understanding of Jesus as the Messianic king who brings divine peace. Spreading cloaks on the road is the way a king was typically greeted; it is a dramatic gesture, considering this outer garment was a person's most valuable piece of clothing, offering protection from the weather and serving as a blanket at night.

The Pharisees, on the other hand, may have been concerned that the disciples' acclamation of Jesus as king would sound like rebellion to the Roman occupiers.

Jesus' lament over Jerusalem was fulfilled in the First Jewish-Roman war (A.D. 66–73), which the first readers of Luke's Gospel would have lived through. Brutal infighting among Jewish factions contributed to the Romans' conquest of Jerusalem in A.D. 70. The Romans first besieged the city, starving the population; then they burned and leveled everything, including the Temple, and slaughtered the inhabitants. According to the Jewish historian Josephus, the streets ran with blood.

Consider …

- Who are you in this story? Are you one of the disciples? A passerby? One of the religious leaders? The colt?
- Imagine the festive procession into Jerusalem. What do you see, smell, and feel? What sounds (singing,

cheering?) do you hear?

- How does Jesus respond to the words and actions of the crowd?

Walk with Jesus

Take a moment to pray for what your heart most desires from this encounter with Jesus.

Then let the Holy Spirit be your guide as you enter the Gospel story.

As you finish walking with Jesus, share your thoughts, feelings, and desires with God, much as one friend would speak to another.

Reflect on the Journey

After you are finished praying, savor and reflect on your experience, either in your prayer journal or with your prayer group. Begin by writing or sharing the story of your imaginative prayer journey: What happened during your time with Jesus? Then consider the following questions:

- How did you accompany Jesus on his way into Jerusalem? Were you right out front, running alongside him, or watching from a distance?
- Jesus enters Jerusalem as the King of Peace. How does this title fit with your experience of him? Does Jesus bring peace into your life?
- How did you feel watching Jesus weep over Jerusalem? What "Jerusalems" do you weep over today?

(28)

Jesus Cleanses the Temple

(Mt 21:12–17)

Walk with Jesus as he enters the temple area, driving out
the merchants and healing the blind and the lame.

Prepare

Take a few moments to quietly welcome God's presence.

Lord, thank you for meeting me here in prayer. Thank you for loving me. Please give me the grace to love and serve you in all my
thoughts, words, and actions.

Jesus, send your Holy Spirit to help me walk with you as you
sanctify your Father's house. Let your Spirit breathe in me, enlivening my imagination so that I can grow closer to you. Amen.

Read

MATTHEW 21:12–17

Then Jesus entered the temple and drove out all who were selling
and buying in the temple, and he overturned the tables of the money changers and the seats of those who sold doves. He said to them,
"It is written:

> 'My house shall be called a house of prayer';
> but you are making it a den of robbers."

The blind and the lame came to him in the temple, and he cured
them. But when the chief priests and the scribes saw the amazing
things that he did, and heard the children crying out in the temple, "Hosanna to the Son of David," they became angry and said to
him, "Do you hear what these are saying?" Jesus said to them, "Yes;
have you never read,

> 'Out of the mouths of infants and nursing babies
>   you have prepared praise for yourself'?"

He left them, went out of the city to Bethany, and spent the night
there.

✠

Set the Scene

This story takes place in the area of the Temple — specifically, the
huge outer Court of the Gentiles, where animals were sold for sacrificial offerings. Rather than transport their animals on the long
journey to Jerusalem, many pilgrims sold an animal at home and
purchased an animal at the Temple. Before they could purchase a
sacrificial animal or pay the Temple tax, though, they needed to
convert their Roman or other foreign currency into Tyrian shekels,
the official currency of the Temple.

In the Gospel of Matthew (and in Mark and Luke), Jesus' action in the Temple takes place immediately before the Passover celebration, when Jerusalem — and the Temple — would have been especially crowded. The Court of the Gentiles would have bustled with thousands of animals, including the sheep necessary for the Passover meal. Doves were sold to those who could not afford a more expensive offering.

Jesus quotes the prophets Isaiah and Jeremiah; his listeners would have known the references. Isaiah 56:7 describes the Temple as "a house of prayer for all peoples," but Gentiles were excluded from the inner courts of the Temple, as were the blind and the lame. Jesus' healing of the blind and the lame would have given them the same access to the Temple as other Jews had.

Children, too, play a role in this drama, announcing the presence of the Messiah in the Temple. The Hebrew word *Hosanna* means "[O Lord], grant salvation."

To help you imagine the setting of the Temple, see "A Brief Tour of First-Century Palestine."

Consider ...

- Who are you in this story? One of the pilgrims? A disciple? A money changer? One of the children? One of those healed by Jesus?
- Imagine the crowded and chaotic setting of the Temple. What do you see and hear? Can you smell the animals? What do you notice about the merchants and the pilgrims?
- What does Jesus' face look like as he drives out the money changers?

Walk with Jesus

Take a moment to pray for what your heart most desires from this encounter with Jesus.

Then let the Holy Spirit be your guide as you enter the Gospel story.

As you finish walking with Jesus, share your thoughts, feelings, and desires with God, much as one friend would speak to another.

Reflect on the Journey

After you are finished praying, savor and reflect on your experience, either in your prayer journal or with your prayer group. Begin by writing or sharing the story of your imaginative prayer journey: What happened during your time with Jesus? Then consider the following questions:

- How do you feel about what Jesus did and the emotions he demonstrated?
- When do you experience righteous frustration, impatience, or anger? Do these emotions ever lead you closer to God?
- How do Jesus' prophetic words and actions speak to your own life today?

(29)

The Anointing of Jesus

(Jn 12:1–8)

Join Jesus and his disciples as they enjoys a celebratory
dinner with Mary, Martha, and Lazarus.

Prepare

Take a few moments to quietly welcome God's presence.

Lord, thank you for meeting me here in prayer. Thank you for loving me. Please give me the grace to love and serve you in all my
thoughts, words, and actions.

Jesus, allow me to join you and your friends for a celebratory
meal. Let your Spirit breathe in me, enlivening my imagination so
that I can grow closer to you. Amen.

Read

JOHN 12:1–8

Six days before the Passover Jesus came to Bethany, the home of Lazarus, whom he had raised from the dead. There they gave a dinner for him. Martha served, and Lazarus was one of those at the table with him. Mary took a pound of costly perfume made of pure nard, anointed Jesus' feet, and wiped them with her hair. The house was filled with the fragrance of the perfume. But Judas Iscariot, one of his disciples (the one who was about to betray him), said, "Why was this perfume not sold for three hundred denarii and the money given to the poor?" (He said this not because he cared about the poor, but because he was a thief; he kept the common purse and used to steal what was put into it.) Jesus said, "Leave her alone. She bought it so that she might keep it for the day of my burial. You always have the poor with you, but you do not always have me."

✠

Set the Scene

This story occurs shortly after Jesus raises Lazarus from the dead (Jn 11:1–44) in the home of Jesus' friends Mary and Martha. The feast of Passover is just six days away, and the Jewish authorities are now actively plotting to kill Jesus.

Nard (or spikenard) is an aromatic oil derived from a plant found in the mountains of northern India. Washing the feet of a guest with water was a custom of hospitality in the ancient Near East; Mary's actions go well above and beyond normal standards of hospitality. Note that the text says she used a pound of this expensive perfume to anoint Jesus before his impending death and burial.

Recall that Mary is accustomed to sitting at the feet of Jesus in the posture of a disciple, and Martha is accustomed to serving (Lk 10:38–42; see reading guide #23).

Jesus' statement about always having the poor among us is a

reference to Deuteronomy 15:11: "Since there will never cease to be some in need on the earth, I therefore command you, 'Open your hand to the poor and needy neighbor in your land.'"

As you read the Gospel of John's version of this story, bear in mind that the other Gospels tell the same story in slightly different ways. The version in the Gospel of Luke is the most unique, and the only one to identify the person anointing Jesus' feet as a sinful woman. Don't saddle Mary of Bethany with the sins of the woman from Luke's Gospel, which some scholars consider to be an altogether separate account.

To help you imagine the setting of the sisters' home, see "A Brief Tour of First-Century Palestine."

Consider …

- Who are you in this story? Mary? Martha? Lazarus? One of the other disciples? Judas?
- Imagine this dinner among friends. What does the food taste like? What kind of clothing do people wear? What is the conversation like? Look at the faces of the other people in the room as Mary anoints Jesus' feet. What range of reactions do you see?
- How does Jesus react to Mary's action? How do you feel toward him?

Walk with Jesus

Take a moment to pray for what your heart most desires from this encounter with Jesus.

Then let the Holy Spirit be your guide as you enter the Gospel story.

As you finish walking with Jesus, share your thoughts, feelings, and desires with God, much as one friend would speak to another.

Reflect on the Journey

After you are finished praying, savor and reflect on your experience, either in your prayer journal or with your prayer group. Begin by writing or sharing the story of your imaginative prayer journey: What happened during your time with Jesus? Then consider the following questions:

- Mary does not hesitate to express her love for Jesus, even in a public setting. How do you express your love and appreciation for the people you know?
- What would it be like for you to "anoint" Jesus as extravagantly as Mary did?
- Judas objects to Mary's extravagance. Do you ever want to hold back from others (or Jesus) for practical reasons?

(30)

The Last Supper

(Lk 22:14–34)

Sit with Jesus as he celebrates the Passover meal with
his disciples on the eve of his Passion and death.

Prepare

Take a few moments to quietly welcome God's presence.

Lord, thank you for meeting me here in prayer. Thank you for loving me. Please give me the grace to love and serve you in all my
thoughts, words, and actions.

Jesus, allow me to sit with you as you celebrate the Passover
meal with your friends. Let your Spirit breathe in me, enlivening
my imagination so that I can grow closer to you. Amen.

Read

LUKE 22:14–34

When the hour came, he took his place at the table, and the apostles with him. He said to them, "I have eagerly desired to eat this Passover with you before I suffer; for I tell you, I will not eat it until it is fulfilled in the kingdom of God." Then he took a cup, and after giving thanks he said, "Take this and divide it among yourselves; for I tell you that from now on I will not drink of the fruit of the vine until the kingdom of God comes." Then he took a loaf of bread, and when he had given thanks, he broke it and gave it to them, saying, "This is my body, which is given for you. Do this in remembrance of me." And he did the same with the cup after supper, saying, "This cup that is poured out for you is the new covenant in my blood. But see, the one who betrays me is with me, and his hand is on the table. For the Son of Man is going as it has been determined, but woe to that one by whom he is betrayed!" Then they began to ask one another which one of them it could be who would do this.

A dispute also arose among them as to which one of them was to be regarded as the greatest. But he said to them, "The kings of the Gentiles lord it over them; and those in authority over them are called benefactors. But not so with you; rather the greatest among you must become like the youngest, and the leader like one who serves. For who is greater, the one who is at the table or the one who serves? Is it not the one at the table? But I am among you as one who serves.

"You are those who have stood by me in my trials; and I confer on you, just as my Father has conferred on me, a kingdom, so that you may eat and drink at my table in my kingdom, and you will sit on thrones judging the twelve tribes of Israel.

"Simon, Simon, listen! Satan has demanded to sift all of you like wheat, but I have prayed for you that your own faith may not fail; and you, when once you have turned back, strengthen your brothers." And he said to him, "Lord, I am ready to go with you to prison and to death!" Jesus said, "I tell you, Peter, the cock will not crow this day, until you have denied three times that you know me."

✠

Set the Scene

This story of how Jesus celebrated the Passover meal with his friends on the night before his death may feel overly familiar: We hear part of this text every time we celebrate the Eucharist, and we have probably seen many paintings of the Last Supper. Try refreshing this important story by imaginatively savoring the physical, sensory reality of the meal.

The meal took place in a large, furnished upper room (Mk 14:15; Lk 22:12); only more affluent people could afford to build a two-story home, so the furnishings may have been more luxurious than typical. Jesus and his friends would have gathered there in the evening before sunset, because the Passover meal begins after sunset. The room would have been lit with oil lamps; if it was cool, a small coal fire may have burned in a metal brazier.

For a formal occasion such as this, servants would usually attend the guests; the presence of servants seems likely if Jesus did not want the twelve apostles to be distracted by the duties of meal preparation and serving. The owner of the home may have supplied servants, or other followers of Jesus may have served Jesus and the Twelve.

Jesus and the disciples would have reclined to eat, probably around a low, U-shaped table called a triclinium. The servants would have stood or sat on stools at the two ends of the U. The host — Jesus — would have taken the second position from the end, with the most honored guest reclining to his right, and the other guests positioned in order of declining stature to his left. The diners would lean on their left elbows to support themselves, freeing their right hands for eating.

The Passover meal was held annually in the spring to commemorate the night when God liberated the Israelites from slavery. The menu included lamb, unleavened bread, vegetables and herbs, vinegar, and four ritual cups of wine.

The food, as well as the prayers and rituals surrounding the meal, recall the Israelites' last evening meal in Egypt before the day of their liberation. The course of the Passover meal was marked by the blessing and drinking of the four ritual cups of wine, each of which would be accompanied by prayers, the singing of psalms, ritual hand washing, and the recitation of one of the four parts of Exodus 6:6–7:

> I am the LORD, and I will free you from the burdens of the Egyptians and deliver you from slavery to them. I will redeem you with an outstretched arm and with mighty acts of judgment. I will take you as my people, and I will be your God. You shall know that I am the LORD your God, who has freed you from the burdens of the Egyptians.

The main part of the meal was eaten between the second and third ritual cups. After the meal, the remaining unleavened bread would be blessed, broken, and eaten. Then the third ritual cup of wine would be blessed, and the third part of Exodus 6:6 would be recited. This third ritual cup, known as the "redemption cup," is the one we most often associate with Jesus' institution of the Eucharist. After the blessing and drinking of the fourth ritual cup, the meal would have concluded with the singing of psalms of thanksgiving.

These details would have been familiar to most of those who originally heard the Gospel, and would have placed Jesus' words at the breaking of the bread and the blessing of the cup within a rich historical and theological context — namely, God's plan to claim and save his people. The simplified description provided here is meant to help you experience the Last Supper more richly. However, for the purposes of imaginative prayer, we do not want to worry too much about accurately re-creating every detail of the Passover meal. Our focus is on being present with Jesus.

Consider ...

- Who are you in this story? One of the disciples? A servant? Or someone else — perhaps a child spying on the adults?
- Imagine yourself entering the upper room before the meal. What does the room look like? Can you smell the food being prepared in the courtyard below? What can you see and hear out the windows? Who is seated near you at the table?
- How does Jesus' mood change throughout the evening?

Walk with Jesus

Take a moment to pray for what your heart most desires from this encounter with Jesus.

Then let the Holy Spirit be your guide as you enter the Gospel story.

As you finish walking with Jesus, share your thoughts, feelings, and desires with God, much as one friend would speak to another.

Reflect on the Journey

After you are finished praying, savor and reflect on your experience, either in your prayer journal or with your prayer group. Begin by writing or sharing the story of your imaginative prayer journey: What happened during your time with Jesus? Then consider the following questions:

- The Last Supper may have been a solemn celebration, but it was also fraught with tension, bickering, and sadness. Do you experience a similar situation anywhere in your own life — for instance, in your parish, workplace, or family?

- Looking back, later Christians would recognize the gift of the Eucharist that Jesus gave to his friends at the Last Supper, but at the time, they seem largely oblivious; they seem more focused on their own concerns. What gifts has Jesus given you? How have you acknowledged those gifts?

- How would your life be different if you fully embraced Jesus' words about humility and service?

(31)

In the Garden of
Gethsemane

(Mt 26:36–46)

Walk with Jesus and his disciples to the Mount of Olives,
where an anguished Jesus will turn to the Father in prayer.

Prepare

Take a few moments to quietly welcome God's presence.

Lord, thank you for meeting me here in prayer. Thank you for loving me. Please give me the grace to love and serve you in all my
thoughts, words, and actions.

Jesus, allow me to join you in prayer In the Garden of Gethsemane. Let your Spirit breathe in me, enlivening my imagination so
that I can grow closer to you. Amen.

Read

MATTHEW 26:36–46

Then Jesus went with them to a place called Gethsemane; and he said to his disciples, "Sit here while I go over there and pray." He took with him Peter and the two sons of Zebedee, and began to be grieved and agitated. Then he said to them, "I am deeply grieved, even to death; remain here, and stay awake with me." And going a little farther, he threw himself on the ground and prayed, "My Father, if it is possible, let this cup pass from me; yet not what I want but what you want." Then he came to the disciples and found them sleeping; and he said to Peter, "So, could you not stay awake with me one hour? Stay awake and pray that you may not come into the time of trial; the spirit indeed is willing, but the flesh is weak." Again he went away for the second time and prayed, "My Father, if this cannot pass unless I drink it, your will be done." Again he came and found them sleeping, for their eyes were heavy. So leaving them again, he went away and prayed for the third time, saying the same words. Then he came to the disciples and said to them, "Are you still sleeping and taking your rest? See, the hour is at hand, and the Son of Man is betrayed into the hands of sinners. Get up, let us be going. See, my betrayer is at hand."

✠

Set the Scene

After finishing the Passover meal, which would have begun shortly after sunset and taken several hours, Jesus and his friends went to Gethsemane, an olive orchard just east of Jerusalem on the Mount of Olives, which overlooked the city.

The Mount of Olives, part of a ridge of low mountains, got its name from the many olive groves covering its slopes. It was also home to a large and ancient Jewish cemetery containing thousands of graves and burial caves dug into formations of soft chalk. The Mount of Olives was supposed to be the place from which the Messiah would enter the city of Jerusalem, and the place where the resurrection of the dead would begin.

The olive grove would have been lit by a full moon (Passover always occurs on the full moon), and the air would have been cool (because Passover occurs in the spring). Olive trees in that area are short and squat, with silver-green leaves and gnarled limbs.

Consider ...

- Who are you in this story? One of the disciples who stay at a distance? One of the three disciples who join Jesus in prayer (and fall asleep)? Or someone else?
- What are the sights, sounds, and smells of this night on the Mount of Olives? Is the full moon out, or is it cloudy? What does Jerusalem look like from here? Can you hear the distant noises of the city?
- What do you notice about Jesus as he prays?

Walk with Jesus

Take a moment to pray for what your heart most desires from this encounter with Jesus.

Then let the Holy Spirit be your guide as you enter the Gospel story.

As you finish walking with Jesus, share your thoughts, feelings, and desires with God, much as one friend would speak to another.

Reflect on the Journey

After you are finished praying, savor and reflect on your experience, either in your prayer journal or with your prayer group. Begin by writing or sharing the story of your imaginative prayer journey: What happened during your time with Jesus? Then consider the following questions:

- How did it make you feel to see Jesus so distressed?

How did you want to comfort Jesus?

- Do you ever "fall asleep" on Jesus? Do you ever feel worn out in your journey with him?
- What is your prayer like when you are "grieved and agitated"?

(32)

Jesus Is Betrayed
and Arrested

(Mk 14:43–52)

Walk with Jesus as an armed crowd comes
to arrest him and his friends flee.

Prepare

Take a few moments to quietly welcome God's presence.

Lord, thank you for meeting me here in prayer. Thank you for loving me. Please give me the grace to love and serve you in all my thoughts, words, and actions.

Jesus, help me stay with you as you are unjustly arrested. Let your Spirit breathe in me, enlivening my imagination so that I can grow closer to you. Amen.

Read

MARK 14:43–52

Immediately, while he was still speaking, Judas, one of the twelve, arrived; and with him there was a crowd with swords and clubs, from the chief priests, the scribes, and the elders. Now the betrayer had given them a sign, saying, "The one I will kiss is the man; arrest him and lead him away under guard." So when he came, he went up to him at once and said, "Rabbi!" and kissed him. Then they laid hands on him and arrested him. But one of those who stood near drew his sword and struck the slave of the high priest, cutting off his ear. Then Jesus said to them, "Have you come out with swords and clubs to arrest me as though I were a bandit? Day after day I was with you in the temple teaching, and you did not arrest me. But let the scriptures be fulfilled." All of them deserted him and fled.

A certain young man was following him, wearing nothing but a linen cloth. They caught hold of him, but he left the linen cloth and ran off naked.

✠

Set the Scene

The setting of this story is an olive grove on the Mount of Olives; see the setting notes for "In the Garden of Gethsemane" (reading guide #31).

The kiss Judas gives to betray Jesus is the customary greeting of a student to his teacher. It is also frequently mentioned in the letters of Paul as a customary greeting among the first Christians.

As for the young man who slips away without his clothes, his identity has been debated for centuries without any clear resolution.

Consider ...

- Who are you in this story? One of the sleepy disciples? Someone in the armed crowd? The young man who runs away naked?

- Where are the shadows and dark places in this scene? Where does the light come from? What is the expression on the faces of Jesus' friends when they see the armed mob?
- What is the expression on Jesus' face when Judas greets him?

Walk with Jesus

Take a moment to pray for what your heart most desires from this encounter with Jesus.

Then let the Holy Spirit be your guide as you enter the Gospel story.

As you finish walking with Jesus, share your thoughts, feelings, and desires with God, much as one friend would speak to another.

Reflect on the Journey

After you are finished praying, savor and reflect on your experience, either in your prayer journal or with your prayer group. Begin by writing or sharing the story of your imaginative prayer journey: What happened during your time with Jesus? Then consider the following questions:

- Have you ever betrayed a friend? Have you ever been betrayed? How does this story connect with that experience?
- How did you react when they arrested Jesus? Did you stay, flee, or fight?
- Have you ever felt abandoned by all your friends? If so, where was God in that experience?

(33)

Peter Denies Jesus

(Lk 22:54–62)

Walk with Jesus as Peter denies knowing
him, not once, but three times.

Prepare

Take a few moments to quietly welcome God's presence.

Lord, thank you for meeting me here in prayer. Thank you for loving me. Please give me the grace to love and serve you in all my
thoughts, words, and actions.

Jesus, allow me to accompany you as your closest friend denies
knowing you. Let your Spirit breathe in me, enlivening my imagination so that I can grow closer to you. Amen.

Read

LUKE 22:54–62

Then they seized him and led him away, bringing him into the high priest's house. But Peter was following at a distance. When they had kindled a fire in the middle of the courtyard and sat down together, Peter sat among them. Then a servant-girl, seeing him in the firelight, stared at him and said, "This man also was with him." But he denied it, saying, "Woman, I do not know him." A little later someone else, on seeing him, said, "You also are one of them." But Peter said, "Man, I am not!" Then about an hour later still another kept insisting, "Surely this man also was with him; for he is a Galilean." But Peter said, "Man, I do not know what you are talking about!" At that moment, while he was still speaking, the cock crowed. The Lord turned and looked at Peter. Then Peter remembered the word of the Lord, how he had said to him, "Before the cock crows today, you will deny me three times." And he went out and wept bitterly.

☦

Set the Scene

The exact route Jesus' captors took from the Garden of Gethsemane to the house of the high priest is not known. However, it is likely that Jesus was led through the Kidron Valley, around the Temple Mount, and through the sleeping city late at night. Peter followed at a distance. Although it was late at night, the city was crowded with pilgrims celebrating the Passover feast, so it is likely that not everyone was asleep. As previously noted, the moon would have been full.

The courtyard in which Peter sat with the servants around a fire would have been the inner courtyard of the high priest's house.

Consider ...

- Who are you in this story? You might imagine yourself

as Peter, sticking to the shadows as you follow Jesus at a safe distance. Or perhaps you are one of the servants who questions Peter, another disciple accompanying Peter, or one of those taking Jesus to the high priest.

- Imagine the city at night. What do you hear in the distance? What do you see in the sky? Who is in the mob leading Jesus to the high priest? Who are the people in the courtyard?
- Imagine the look Jesus gives Peter after the cock crows. What does that look communicate?

Walk with Jesus

Take a moment to pray for what your heart most desires from this encounter with Jesus.

Then let the Holy Spirit be your guide as you enter the Gospel story.

As you finish walking with Jesus, share your thoughts, feelings, and desires with God, much as one friend would speak to another.

Reflect on the Journey

After you are finished praying, savor and reflect on your experience, either in your prayer journal or with your prayer group. Begin by writing or sharing the story of your imaginative prayer journey: What happened during your time with Jesus? Then consider the following questions:

- Have you ever denied Jesus?
- "The Lord turned and looked at Peter" (Lk 22:61). How did you interpret that look? Has Jesus ever "looked" at you in this way?
- Have you ever been mocked, ridiculed, or reviled for your association with someone else? Have you ever been treated this way because you know Jesus?

(34)

Jesus before Pilate

(Mk 15:1–20)

Accompany Jesus as he is questioned by Pilate
and then mocked and scourged.

Prepare

Take a few moments to quietly welcome God's presence.

Lord, thank you for meeting me here in prayer. Thank you for loving me. Please give me the grace to love and serve you in all my
thoughts, words, and actions.

Jesus, let me bear witness to your trial and scourging. Let your
Spirit breathe in me, enlivening my imagination so that I can grow
closer to you. Amen.

Read

MARK 15:1–20

As soon as it was morning, the chief priests held a consultation with the elders and scribes and the whole council. They bound Jesus, led him away, and handed him over to Pilate. Pilate asked him, "Are you the King of the Jews?" He answered him, "You say so." Then the chief priests accused him of many things. Pilate asked him again, "Have you no answer? See how many charges they bring against you." But Jesus made no further reply, so that Pilate was amazed.

Now at the festival he used to release a prisoner for them, anyone for whom they asked. Now a man called Barabbas was in prison with the rebels who had committed murder during the insurrection. So the crowd came and began to ask Pilate to do for them according to his custom. Then he answered them, "Do you want me to release for you the King of the Jews?" For he realized that it was out of jealousy that the chief priests had handed him over. But the chief priests stirred up the crowd to have him release Barabbas for them instead. Pilate spoke to them again, "Then what do you wish me to do with the man you call the King of the Jews?" They shouted back, "Crucify him!" Pilate asked them, "Why? what evil has he done?" But they shouted all the more, "Crucify him!" So Pilate, wishing to satisfy the crowd, released Barabbas for them; and after flogging Jesus, he handed him over to be crucified.

Then the soldiers led him into the courtyard of the palace (that is, the governor's headquarters); and they called together the whole cohort. And they clothed him in a purple cloak; and after twisting some thorns into a crown, they put it on him. And they began saluting him, "Hail, King of the Jews!" They struck his head with a reed, spat upon him, and knelt down in homage to him. After mocking him, they stripped him of the purple cloak and put his own clothes on him. Then they led him out to crucify him.

✠

Set the Scene

The Sanhedrin was a council of seventy-one elders who functioned as a sort of supreme court; they met every day except on festivals and the Sabbath. They met in the Hall of Hewn Stones, attached to the Temple.

Pontius Pilate was the Roman prefect of Judea from A.D. 26 to 36; he was often in conflict with the Jewish population. On this occasion, he was probably visiting Jerusalem in order to keep an eye on the crowds gathered for the Passover feast.

The trial of Jesus before Pontius Pilate is traditionally thought to have occurred at the Antonia Fortress, a one-hundred-foot-high citadel overlooking the Temple area and housing a garrison of Roman soldiers. However, recent scholars say there is much stronger evidence for the trial taking place at Herod's palace, a huge complex that was second in size and opulence only to the Temple.

A trial at the palace would have occurred in the praetorium, the residence of the Roman governor when he was visiting Jerusalem. The building would have resembled a large Roman home, with plastered walls, archways, and columns; a schedule of fees and taxes was often carved directly into the walls.

Wherever the trial took place, people present may have included servants, guards, and other Roman and Jewish government officials.

Pilate's questioning of Jesus focuses on his supposed claim to be the King of the Jews, a claim that Roman authorities would have viewed as threatening their own rule. The Gospel of Mark presumes, but does not mention, that Pilate issued a guilty verdict before asking the crowds whether they wanted him to release Jesus or Barabbas, a Jewish revolutionary.

A public scourging preceded crucifixion. The victim would be stripped naked, tied to a pillar, and then whipped across the back, buttocks, and legs with leather straps containing sharp pieces of bone or metal that tore deep into the flesh. The resulting severe pain and blood loss often caused victims to faint or even die.

Consider ...

- Who are you in this story? A Roman official? A servant? A member of the Sanhedrin? Someone else?
- Imagine the setting of Jesus' trial. What is it like inside when Pilate is questioning him? How many people are in the crowd, and what do they sound like as they demand Jesus' death? What range of emotions do you see on others' faces? Boredom, incredulity, pity, loathing?
- What do you notice about Jesus' eyes? How do you feel toward Jesus?
- This story includes at least three scenes: Jesus before the Sanhedrin, Jesus before Pilate, and Jesus being scourged and mocked by the soldiers. You may wish to focus on just one scene.

Walk with Jesus

Take a moment to pray for what your heart most desires from this encounter with Jesus.

Then let the Holy Spirit be your guide as you enter the Gospel story.

As you finish walking with Jesus, share your thoughts, feelings, and desires with God, much as one friend would speak to another.

Reflect on the Journey

After you are finished praying, savor and reflect on your experience, either in your prayer journal or with your prayer group. Begin by writing or sharing the story of your imaginative prayer journey: What happened during your time with Jesus? Then consider the following questions:

- This story turns on the title "King of the Jews." Do you

ever relate to Jesus as a king?

- "Crucify him!" (Mk 15:13). Pilate is ready to release Jesus, but the crowd demands his death. In your life, do you tend to follow the crowd? Do the "crowds" in your life bring you closer to Jesus or separate you from him?
- Have you ever witnessed someone you love suffering and been powerless to help them? Where was Jesus in that experience?

(35)

The Way of the Cross

(Lk 23:26–32)

Walk with Jesus as he is led away to his death and a man named Simon is made to follow him, carrying the cross.

Prepare
Take a few moments to quietly welcome God's presence.

Lord, thank you for meeting me here in prayer. Thank you for loving me. Please give me the grace to love and serve you in all my thoughts, words, and actions.

Jesus, let me walk with you on the way to your crucifixion. Let your Spirit breathe in me, enlivening my imagination so that I can grow closer to you. Amen.

Read

LUKE 23:26–32

As they led him away, they seized a man, Simon of Cyrene, who was coming from the country, and they laid the cross on him, and made him carry it behind Jesus. A great number of the people followed him, and among them were women who were beating their breasts and wailing for him. But Jesus turned to them and said, "Daughters of Jerusalem, do not weep for me, but weep for yourselves and for your children. For the days are surely coming when they will say, 'Blessed are the barren, and the wombs that never bore, and the breasts that never nursed.' Then they will begin to say to the mountains, 'Fall on us'; and to the hills, 'Cover us.' For if they do this when the wood is green, what will happen when it is dry?"

Two others also, who were criminals, were led away to be put to death with him.

✠

Set the Scene

Victims of crucifixion were typically made to carry the patibulum, or crossbeam, to the site of the crucifixion. Walking barefoot over uneven paving stones and weakened by the flogging, they were likely to fall along the way. If they did fall, they could not catch themselves, because their arms were tied to the crossbeam. Moreover, victims often had to move through the crowded streets sideways, exposing their genitals and kidneys to the kicks and punches of people in the crowd.

It was fortunate for Jesus, then, that Simon of Cyrene was chosen to carry the crossbeam for at least part of the way. Cyrene was a city in northern Africa (in present-day Libya) with a large population of Judean Jews. These Jews had their own synagogue in Jerusalem, which they visited on important feast days. Simon was likely in Jerusalem to celebrate the Passover festival.

The route Jesus took is unknown, but he would have walked

anywhere from a quarter of a mile to almost a mile on the way to his death. As he exited Jerusalem, he stopped to address the women who were following him. In the Gospel of Luke, this speech forms a bookend to his lament over Jerusalem upon his entering the city before the Passover.

Consider …

- Who are you in this story? Are you Simon of Cyrene? One of the women following Jesus? One of the soldiers? An anonymous face in the crowd?
- What do you see, hear, and smell as you follow Jesus on the way to Calvary? Imagine the crowded streets, the city gate, the place of execution. Whose faces stand out?
- What do you notice about Jesus' face? How do you feel toward him?

Walk with Jesus

Take a moment to pray for what your heart most desires from this encounter with Jesus.

Then let the Holy Spirit be your guide as you enter the Gospel story.

As you finish walking with Jesus, share your thoughts, feelings, and desires with God, much as one friend would speak to another.

Reflect on the Journey

After you are finished praying, savor and reflect on your experience, either in your prayer journal or with your prayer group. Begin by writing or sharing the story of your imaginative prayer journey: What happened during your time with Jesus? Then consider the following questions:

- Have you ever carried someone else's cross? What

came of that for you?
- What is the most difficult journey you have ever made — your own "way of the cross"?
- Has anyone ever helped you through a period of difficulty and suffering? Looking back, can you see Jesus in that experience?

(36)

The Crucifixion of Jesus

(Lk 23:33–43)

Accompany Jesus as he is crucified alongside
two criminals and mocked by the crowds.

Prepare
Take a few moments to quietly welcome God's presence.

Lord, thank you for meeting me here in prayer. Thank you for loving me. Please give me the grace to love and serve you in all my
thoughts, words, and actions.

Jesus, allow me to stand at the foot of your cross as I bear witness to your suffering and humiliation. Let your Spirit breathe in
me, enlivening my imagination so that I can grow closer to you.
Amen.

Read

Luke 23:33–43

When they came to the place that is called The Skull, they crucified Jesus there with the criminals, one on his right and one on his left. [[Then Jesus said, "Father, forgive them; for they do not know what they are doing."]] And they cast lots to divide his clothing. And the people stood by, watching; but the leaders scoffed at him, saying, "He saved others; let him save himself if he is the Messiah of God, his chosen one!" The soldiers also mocked him, coming up and offering him sour wine, and saying, "If you are the King of the Jews, save yourself!" There was also an inscription over him, "This is the King of the Jews."

One of the criminals who were hanged there kept deriding him and saying, "Are you not the Messiah? Save yourself and us!" But the other rebuked him, saying, "Do you not fear God, since you are under the same sentence of condemnation? And we indeed have been condemned justly, for we are getting what we deserve for our deeds, but this man has done nothing wrong." Then he said, "Jesus, remember me when you come into your kingdom." He replied, "Truly I tell you, today you will be with me in Paradise."

✠

Set the Scene

Thousands of people, including (occasionally) women and children, were executed by crucifixion throughout the Mediterranean over a period of about five hundred years. In the Roman Empire, crucifixion was reserved for rebellious slaves and enemies of the state, and served as a gruesome public warning to others who might consider opposing Rome.

After arriving at the place of execution, the victim would be stripped naked and nailed to the patibulum (crossbeam), which was then lifted and attached to an upright post; his feet were then tied or nailed to the post. In Jerusalem, victims were sometimes offered a pain-relieving drink made of wine and myrrh.

The word *excruciating* comes from the practice of crucifixion (meaning "from the cross"). Besides the pain from the nails and the preceding scourging, hanging from the cross slowly weakened the muscles used for breathing; thus, most victims died of asphyxiation. It took anywhere between a few hours and a few days for victims to die.

According to the Bible, Jesus' crucifixion took place just outside the walls of the city. Aside from those who came specifically to witness the spectacle, others entering and leaving the city — including the many pilgrims traveling for the Passover festival — would have passed by the site. Later in the Gospel, Luke says that all Jesus' acquaintances, including his women followers, observed these events from a distance (Lk 23:49).

Consider …

- Who are you in this story? One of Jesus' friends, watching from a distance? One of the men crucified with him? One of the soldiers? A passerby?
- What do you see and smell in the area of the crucifixion? Who passes by on the road to Jerusalem? Whose voices do you hear? What expressions do you see on the faces of the onlookers?
- What do you notice about the crucified Jesus?

Walk with Jesus

Take a moment to pray for what your heart most desires from this encounter with Jesus.

Then let the Holy Spirit be your guide as you enter the Gospel story.

As you finish walking with Jesus, share your thoughts, feelings, and desires with God, much as one friend would speak to another.

Reflect on the Journey

After you are finished praying, savor and reflect on your experience, either in your prayer journal or with your prayer group. Begin by writing or sharing the story of your imaginative prayer journey: What happened during your time with Jesus? Then consider the following questions:

- Do you ever struggle with offering or receiving forgiveness? Can you hear Jesus' words of forgiveness and reconciliation directed to you?
- Think of the two criminals crucified alongside Jesus. What are they like? In your own life, have you ever felt Jesus compassionately suffering alongside you?
- Were you able to imagine Jesus' suffering, or did you look away? Can you see his face in the suffering of others?

The Death and Burial of Jesus

(Lk 23:44–56)

Accompany Jesus as he surrenders his life to his
Father; walk with his friends, too, as they collect
Jesus' body and lay it in a rock-hewn tomb.

Prepare

Take a few moments to quietly welcome God's presence.

Lord, thank you for meeting me here in prayer. Thank you for loving me. Please give me the grace to love and serve you in all my
thoughts, words, and actions.

Jesus, help me bear witness to your death and burial. Let your
Spirit breathe in me, enlivening my imagination so that I can grow

187

closer to you. Amen.

Read

LUKE 23:44–56

It was now about noon, and darkness came over the whole land until three in the afternoon, while the sun's light failed; and the curtain of the temple was torn in two. Then Jesus, crying with a loud voice, said, "Father, into your hands I commend my spirit." Having said this, he breathed his last. When the centurion saw what had taken place, he praised God and said, "Certainly this man was innocent." And when all the crowds who had gathered there for this spectacle saw what had taken place, they returned home, beating their breasts. But all his acquaintances, including the women who had followed him from Galilee, stood at a distance, watching these things.

Now there was a good and righteous man named Joseph, who, though a member of the council, had not agreed to their plan and action. He came from the Jewish town of Arimathea, and he was waiting expectantly for the kingdom of God. This man went to Pilate and asked for the body of Jesus. Then he took it down, wrapped it in a linen cloth, and laid it in a rock-hewn tomb where no one had ever been laid. It was the day of Preparation, and the sabbath was beginning. The women who had come with him from Galilee followed, and they saw the tomb and how his body was laid. Then they returned, and prepared spices and ointments.

On the sabbath they rested according to the commandment.

✠

Set the Scene

Jesus' cry before his death quotes Psalm 31, which the Jews witnessing the scene would have known by heart:

Into your hand I commit my spirit;

you have redeemed me, O LORD, faithful God. (Psalm
31:5)

The signs that accompany Jesus' death — the darkness as well as
the tearing of the curtain of the inner sanctuary of the Temple —
testify to his true identity.

Little is known about Joseph of Arimathea, other than what
the Gospels tell us: He was a rich man, a member of the Sanhedrin
who had opposed its condemnation of Jesus. According to the Gospel of John, the tomb Jesus was laid in belonged to this holy man.

Jesus died on a Friday, the "Day of Preparation" for the Sabbath,
and so he was buried quickly, probably shortly before sundown.

The more affluent citizens of Jerusalem were commonly buried in caves; the soft, chalklike rock of the region made it easy to dig
out such burial caves. These caves typically had rock shelves carved
on three sides; bodies were placed on these shelves, or on the floor,
with several generations of one family often buried in the same
cave. The cave in which Jesus' body was laid was new, however.

The speed of the burial before the Sabbath prevented Jesus'
women disciples from completing the preparation of his body.

Consider ...

- Who are you in this story? One of the women followers of Jesus, perhaps? Joseph of Arimathea? The centurion? Another bystander?
- What do you see, hear, and smell around the tomb? Is it noisy or quiet? What is the light like, late in the day?
- What do you notice about Jesus' body?

Walk with Jesus

Take a moment to pray for what your heart most desires from this
encounter with Jesus.

Then let the Holy Spirit be your guide as you enter the Gospel story.

As you finish walking with Jesus, share your thoughts, feelings, and desires with God, much as one friend would speak to another.

Reflect on the Journey

After you are finished praying, savor and reflect on your experience, either in your prayer journal or with your prayer group. Begin by writing or sharing the story of your imaginative prayer journey: What happened during your time with Jesus? Then consider the following questions:

- Has Jesus ever felt "dead" in your own life? Have you ever lost faith in him, as some of his followers might have after his death?
- What thoughts and feelings does this prayer experience evoke about your own death and burial? What do you hope it will be like?
- What do you need to do to mourn the death of a loved one? How does this experience of Jesus' death and burial connect to your personal experience?

(38)

The Resurrection of Jesus

(Mt 28:1–10)

Accompany two of the women who have followed
Jesus as they go to his tomb on the morning after
the Sabbath — and encounter the risen Lord.

Prepare

Take a few moments to quietly welcome God's presence.

Lord, thank you for meeting me here in prayer. Thank you for loving me. Please give me the grace to love and serve you in all my thoughts, words, and actions.

Jesus, help me walk with your friends as they discover your empty tomb and encounter you in your Resurrection. Let your Spirit breathe in me, enlivening my imagination so that I can grow closer to you. Amen.

Read

MATTHEW 28:1–10

After the sabbath, as the first day of the week was dawning, Mary Magdalene and the other Mary went to see the tomb. And suddenly there was a great earthquake; for an angel of the Lord, descending from heaven, came and rolled back the stone and sat on it. His appearance was like lightning, and his clothing white as snow. For fear of him the guards shook and became like dead men. But the angel said to the women, "Do not be afraid; I know that you are looking for Jesus who was crucified. He is not here; for he has been raised, as he said. Come, see the place where he lay. Then go quickly and tell his disciples, 'He has been raised from the dead, and indeed he is going ahead of you to Galilee; there you will see him.' This is my message for you." So they left the tomb quickly with fear and great joy, and ran to tell his disciples. Suddenly Jesus met them and said, "Greetings!" And they came to him, took hold of his feet, and worshiped him. Then Jesus said to them, "Do not be afraid; go and tell my brothers to go to Galilee; there they will see me."

Set the Scene

After the Sabbath is concluded, Mary Magdalene and Mary the mother of James and Joseph go to the tomb for the purpose of anointing the body. The guards at the tomb were placed there by Pilate at the request of the Jewish authorities (Mt 27:62–66).

Consider …

- Who are you in this story? One of the two women going out to the tomb? One of the guards? Some unnamed witness?
- Imagine the area of the tomb just after daybreak. What do you see, hear, and feel as you go to the tomb? What morning sounds do you hear? What are the air

and light like?

- What is the resurrected Jesus like? How does he seem different from the Jesus you have imagined in other stories? How does he seem the same?

Walk with Jesus

Take a moment to pray for what your heart most desires from this encounter with Jesus.

Then let the Holy Spirit be your guide as you enter the Gospel story.

As you finish walking with Jesus, share your thoughts, feelings, and desires with God, much as one friend would speak to another.

Reflect on the Journey

After you are finished praying, savor and reflect on your experience, either in your prayer journal or with your prayer group. Begin by writing or sharing the story of your imaginative prayer journey: What happened during your time with Jesus? Then consider the following questions:

- These women went out at dawn to tend to Jesus' body; instead, they became the privileged first witnesses of the Resurrection: "I know that you are looking for Jesus who was crucified. He is not here." (Mt 28:5–6). How do you seek Jesus? Where do you go, and what do you do?
- Has God ever said to you, "Do not be afraid!"? What was that like?
- Have you ever experienced a dramatic "resurrection" in your own life? Or has Jesus ever suddenly "appeared" to you?

(39)

On the Road to Emmaus

(Lk 24:13–35)

Walk with the resurrected Jesus as he journeys with two
of his disciples on the road from Jerusalem to Emmaus.

Prepare

Take a few moments to quietly welcome God's presence.

Lord, thank you for meeting me here in prayer. Thank you for loving me. Please give me the grace to love and serve you in all my
thoughts, words, and actions.

Jesus, help me walk with you on the road to Emmaus. Let your
Spirit breathe in me, enlivening my imagination so that I can grow
closer to you. Amen.

Read

LUKE 24:13–35

Now on that same day two of them were going to a village called Emmaus, about seven miles from Jerusalem, and talking with each other about all these things that had happened. While they were talking and discussing, Jesus himself came near and went with them, but their eyes were kept from recognizing him. And he said to them, "What are you discussing with each other while you walk along?" They stood still, looking sad. Then one of them, whose name was Cleopas, answered him, "Are you the only stranger in Jerusalem who does not know the things that have taken place there in these days?" He asked them, "What things?" They replied, "The things about Jesus of Nazareth, who was a prophet mighty in deed and word before God and all the people, and how our chief priests and leaders handed him over to be condemned to death and crucified him. But we had hoped that he was the one to redeem Israel. Yes, and besides all this, it is now the third day since these things took place. Moreover, some women of our group astounded us. They were at the tomb early this morning, and when they did not find his body there, they came back and told us that they had indeed seen a vision of angels who said that he was alive. Some of those who were with us went to the tomb and found it just as the women had said; but they did not see him." Then he said to them, "Oh, how foolish you are, and how slow of heart to believe all that the prophets have declared! Was it not necessary that the Messiah should suffer these things and then enter into his glory?" Then beginning with Moses and all the prophets, he interpreted to them the things about himself in all the scriptures.

As they came near the village to which they were going, he walked ahead as if he were going on. But they urged him strongly, saying, "Stay with us, because it is almost evening and the day is now nearly over." So he went in to stay with them. When he was at the table with them, he took bread, blessed and broke it, and gave it to them. Then their eyes were opened, and they recognized him; and he vanished from their sight. They said to each other, "Were not our hearts burning within us while he was talking to us on the road, while he was opening the scriptures to us?" That same hour they got up and returned to Jerusalem; and they found the eleven and their companions gathered together. They were saying, "The Lord has risen indeed, and he has appeared to Simon!" Then they told what had happened on the road, and how he had been made known to them in the breaking of the bread.

✠

Set the Scene

This resurrection appearance happens later in the day on Easter Sunday; the two disciples are traveling from Jerusalem to Emmaus, for reasons that are not explained. Presumably, at least one of them has a home there, or at least a place to stay. Scholars have speculated that the unnamed disciple may have been a woman.

Nothing is known about Emmaus; it may have been a small village or hamlet. If so, the "road" to Emmaus may have been more of a footpath.

The disciples' return to Jerusalem — a distance of seven miles — would have taken place at least partly at night. The fact that they would travel by night suggests the urgency they felt.

Consider ...

- You will probably be one of the two disciples in this story. Spend some time providing a "backstory" for them: Who are they? How do they know each other? Why are they leaving Jerusalem? What awaits them in Emmaus?
- Imagine the way to Emmaus. What do you see, hear, and smell as you walk with your companion?
- What does the "stranger" who joins you on your jour-

ney look like? How do you feel toward him at different stages in the journey?

Walk with Jesus

Take a moment to pray for what your heart most desires from this encounter with Jesus.

Then let the Holy Spirit be your guide as you enter the Gospel story.

As you finish walking with Jesus, share your thoughts, feelings, and desires with God, much as one friend would speak to another.

Reflect on the Journey

After you are finished praying, savor and reflect on your experience, either in your prayer journal or with your prayer group. Begin by writing or sharing the story of your imaginative prayer journey: What happened during your time with Jesus? Then consider the following questions:

- "Oh, how foolish you are, and how slow of heart to believe," Jesus says to the two disciples before explaining everything to them (Lk 24:25). What do you want to ask Jesus?
- Do you recognize the risen Jesus, walking alongside you? What prevents that recognition? What opens your eyes to his presence?
- How were the disciples changed by encountering the risen Christ? How has encountering Jesus changed you?

(40)

Jesus Forgives Peter

(Jn 21:1–19)

Accompany Peter and some of Jesus' other disciples as they encounter the risen Jesus on the shore of the Sea of Galilee.

Prepare

Take a few moments to quietly welcome God's presence.

Lord, thank you for meeting me here in prayer. Thank you for loving me. Please give me the grace to love and serve you in all my thoughts, words, and actions.

Jesus, allow me to encounter you in the morning on the shore of the Sea of Galilee. Let your Spirit breathe in me, enlivening my imagination so that I can grow closer to you. Amen.

Read

JOHN 21:1–19

After these things Jesus showed himself again to the disciples by the Sea of Tiberias; and he showed himself in this way. Gathered there together were Simon Peter, Thomas called the Twin, Nathanael of Cana in Galilee, the sons of Zebedee, and two others of his disciples. Simon Peter said to them, "I am going fishing." They said to him, "We will go with you." They went out and got into the boat, but that night they caught nothing.

Just after daybreak, Jesus stood on the beach; but the disciples did not know that it was Jesus. Jesus said to them, "Children, you have no fish, have you?" They answered him, "No." He said to them, "Cast the net to the right side of the boat, and you will find some." So they cast it, and now they were not able to haul it in because there were so many fish. That disciple whom Jesus loved said to Peter, "It is the Lord!" When Simon Peter heard that it was the Lord, he put on some clothes, for he was naked, and jumped into the sea. But the other disciples came in the boat, dragging the net full of fish, for they were not far from the land, only about a hundred yards off.

When they had gone ashore, they saw a charcoal fire there, with fish on it, and bread. Jesus said to them, "Bring some of the fish that you have just caught." So Simon Peter went aboard and hauled the net ashore, full of large fish, a hundred fifty-three of them; and though there were so many, the net was not torn. Jesus said to them, "Come and have breakfast." Now none of the disciples dared to ask him, "Who are you?" because they knew it was the Lord. Jesus came and took the bread and gave it to them, and did the same with the fish. This was now the third time that Jesus appeared to the disciples after he was raised from the dead.

When they had finished breakfast, Jesus said to Simon Peter, "Simon son of John, do you love me more than these?" He said to him, "Yes, Lord; you know that I love you." Jesus said to him, "Feed my lambs." A second time he said to him, "Simon son of John, do you love me?" He said to him, "Yes, Lord; you know that I love you." Jesus said to him, "Tend my sheep." He said to him the third time, "Simon son of John, do you love me?" Peter felt hurt because he said to him the third time, "Do you love me?" And he said to him, "Lord, you know everything; you know that I love you." Jesus said to him, "Feed my sheep. Very truly, I tell you, when you were younger, you used to fasten your own belt and to go wherever you wished. But when you grow old, you will stretch out your hands, and someone else will fasten a belt around you and take you where you do not wish to go." (He said this to indicate the kind of death by which he would glorify God.) After this he said to him, "Follow me."

✠

Set the Scene

Jesus has appeared to these disciples two times already (see John 20:19–29). This third appearance takes place in a familiar setting: the shore of the Sea of Galilee (here called the Sea of Tiberias). The text does not provide the exact location, but if they took Peter's boat, then the disciples may have been gathered at his home in Capernaum.

Fishing was typically done at night so that the fish would not see and avoid the linen or flax nets. A typical fishing boat of the time was shallow-drafted and flat-bottomed, about twenty-seven feet long and seven feet wide, with a mast for a sail and oars for rowing.

The exchange between Jesus and Peter is connected to Peter's threefold denial of Jesus by another charcoal fire (Jn 18:15–18, 25–27; see also reading guide #33, "Peter Denies Jesus").

Consider ...

- Which of the seven disciples are you in this story?
- Imagine the seven disciples fishing as the sun rises

over the sea. What are the air and light like? What do you see on the beach? What can you smell?
- What does the resurrected Jesus look like? What is his posture as he speaks to Peter?

Walk with Jesus

Take a moment to pray for what your heart most desires from this encounter with Jesus.

Then let the Holy Spirit be your guide as you enter the Gospel story.

As you finish walking with Jesus, share your thoughts, feelings, and desires with God, much as one friend would speak to another.

Reflect on the Journey

After you are finished praying, savor and reflect on your experience, either in your prayer journal or with your prayer group. Begin by writing or sharing the story of your imaginative prayer journey: What happened during your time with Jesus? Then consider the following questions:

- Peter recognizes Jesus in the miraculous catch of fish. What signs does Jesus give you about his presence in your life?
- How does the way Jesus reconciles with Peter compare with your own experiences of reconciliation?
- The resurrected Jesus gives Peter a special commission. What special work or mission has Jesus given you to do?

At the End of the Journey

Your journey through the Gospels with Jesus is finished — for now, anyway. Where has it taken you? And how has it changed you?

Take some time now to reflect on these questions:

- What did you learn about Jesus that surprised you?
- How has your image of Jesus changed over the course of this journey? Has your relationship with him changed? How?
- What have you learned about yourself?
- What do you think Jesus is asking you to do now?
- What would you like to say to Jesus?

Walk with Jesus Again

Our journey with Jesus is never really "finished," of course. And if you have found the practice of imaginative prayer to be fruitful, then you may want to try it again in the future. Here are some ways you can continue "walking with Jesus" through the practice of imaginative prayer.

Return to these stories again. Many people find that their experience of a particular Gospel account changes over time; different circumstances or life experiences will change the way you interact with Jesus, for example. Try making it a tradition to return to certain stories once a year, perhaps during an annual retreat or a particular liturgical season, such as Advent, Lent, Holy Week, or Easter.

Journal ... or start a "Walking with Jesus" prayer group. If you went through this book with a small group, or on your own without writing out your experience, try going through it again — but this time, keep a journal. You will be surprised at how recording your experience in writing will lead to new insights.

If you went through this book on your own, try going through it again with a small group. You might form a "Walking with Jesus" prayer group at your church, for example. Check out "How to Organize and Run a 'Walking with Jesus' Prayer Group" on page 215.

Explore more stories about Jesus. The forty stories that form the body of this book do not exhaust all the possibilities, of course. See "Thirty More Readings for Imaginative Prayer" on page 233.

Mix up the text. You might also mix things up by reading a parallel story in a different Gospel (where possible), or by reading a different translation of the Bible. The translation used in this text is the *New Revised Standard Version — Catholic Edition*. Other translations approved by the United States Conference of Catholic Bishops (USCCB) include:

- *New American Bible, Revised Edition*
- *Contemporary English Version — New Testament, First Edition*, American Bible Society
- *So You May Believe, A Translation of the Four Gospels*, Alba House
- *Good News Translation* (Today's English Version, Second Edition), American Bible Society

You can get a complete list from the USCCB website. Many of these translations are available at the Bible Gateway website (not associated with the USCCB).

Walk with Jesus in his hidden life. The public ministry of Jesus recorded in the Gospels was only a small fraction of his life. The *Catechism of the Catholic Church* affirms that the whole of Jesus' life was a revelation of the Father and a mystery of redemption: "During the greater part of his life Jesus shared the condition of the vast majority of human beings: a daily life spent without evident greatness, a life of manual labor" (531). This hidden life of Jesus "allows everyone to enter into fellowship with Jesus by the most ordinary events of daily life" (533).

After you have spent some time with the person of Jesus in the Gospels, try spending time with him in the ordinary events of his daily life. Are you a stay-at-home parent? Try accompanying Mary and the child Jesus (and the other children in the neighborhood) in imaginative prayer. Are you self-employed? Try walking with Jesus as he trades his skill and labor for wages.

Walk with the saints. When St. Ignatius of Loyola was recovering from his war wound, he meditated not only on the life of Christ in the Gospels, but also on the lives and adventures of the saints. If you have a favorite saint, find a good story about that saint and use it as a subject of imaginative prayer. As you walk with your friend the saint, think about how this holy person and the adventure you share together connects you to the Lord.

• • •

At the end of the Gospel of John, the evangelist notes that his Gospel could have many "sequels": "But there are also many other things that Jesus did; if every one of them were written down, I suppose that the world itself could not contain the books that would be written" (Jn 21:25).

Your own walk with Jesus is among the many "books" being written about all that Jesus has done in the world. How will it turn out? You will have to read to the last page to know for sure, but with Jesus at your side, it is sure to be a happy ending!

Five Examples of Imaginative Prayer

To help you get a sense of the "flow and feel" of imaginative prayer, here are some written examples. As I noted in the introduction, writing out your prayer experience is optional; and if you do write it out, you do not need to worry about it being polished. These examples are meant to serve as inspiration, not as a strict template. Notice, however, how each writer composed the setting of the Gospel story with specific details and used that setting for a personal encounter with Jesus.

You can find more written examples of imaginative prayer at gracewatch.org/imagine.

Jesus and the little children

The following reflection is by Julia Walsh, a Franciscan Sister of Perpetual Adoration and part of a new generation of Catholic sisters. She serves as a jail minister and spiritual director in Chicago. Her writing can be found in National Catholic Reporter, America, *and elsewhere. She blogs and podcasts at MessyJesusBusiness.com.*

I hear the disciples bickering with each other, their insecurities twisting their faces into frowns. Their eyebrows are crunched with confusion. Each of them is full of longing: longing to understand the Truth, longing for recognition. Even adults want to feel special, valued, noticed. And we all wonder what is needed to know greatness. Who is the greatest?

Nearby, I see the children laughing and chasing each other, crawling through the dust under some bushes. Their dark, tangled hair is decorated with tiny twigs and leaves. One of them has something smeared on their face — leftover lunch perhaps. The children squeal with joy as they play, seemingly unaware of the adults talking.

Then, Jesus turns and speaks to one of the children, his voice warm with gentle love, "Come here." The child turns, sees Jesus' kind face, and brightens with delight. He jumps into Jesus' wide-open arms, and then Jesus swings him up into the air. The two of them are laughing, caught in a moment of play. The other adults, however, stand around staring. They're confused and surprised.

Jesus holds the child close to his chest. The child is close enough to smell Jesus: a mix of sawdust, herbs, oil, wine, grains, and dust. They both are giggling.

"Become like a child," Jesus tells the adults, who are silently watching the two. "Humble yourself, then you'll be great." As Jesus says this, he taps the child's nose.

I am nearby, sitting on a stump — a quiet observer. I am not yet aware of Jesus' greatness, but I feel my body fill with excitement and attraction. Who is this man that both delights children and informs adults? How can I get to know him? What could he teach me? How can I experience his attention and be as close to him as that sweet child?

Blind Bartimaeus

The following reflection is by Rachelle Linner, a freelance writer, reviewer, and spiritual director who is a frequent contributor to Give Us This Day.

This morning I prayed with the Bartimaeus passage from Mark. At first, I tried to imagine myself one of the crowd, but that was too much like watching the Gospel from outside, so I decided to pray as if I were Bartimaeus.

It was easy for me to relate to him, sitting by the side of the road. I wondered if I would have been angry or depressed if I was in his situation. I am so dependent on sight, even with my visual problems, that the idea of being blind frightens me. And to have to rely on begging so I could buy food and pay for housing! I imagined myself sitting there and suddenly thought of the man who begs outside my parish church on Sundays. I almost always give him some money, but I rarely think of him the rest of the week. But today, because I was imagining myself to be Bartimaeus, I found myself wondering if he ever got angry when people passed by him. Did he feel invisible? It is the thing I hate most, to feel invisible. I hate it when people see me but don't see me. But when I started to call out to Jesus, I was no longer invisible! People started paying attention to me! I remembered what I had heard about Jesus and suddenly knew I would ask him for my greatest desire: to be seen. Not to be ignored, invisible, and irrelevant, but to be seen. I remembered how moved I was when I read Hagar's cry "You are a God who sees!" I long to be seen that way.

And then Jesus called me, and I was overwhelmed — I jumped up and threw off my cloak and felt braver than I ever have in my life. I almost wept when he asked me "What do you want me to do for you?" and I was shocked that I blurted out, "Lord, I want to see." No, I thought, I want to be seen. But I realized it was true. I do want to see. I want to see others the way Jesus sees them. Maybe if I learn to see others like Jesus sees, then, in time, perhaps people will look at me with the same loving gaze. I was so happy that this prayer was given to me. Because it is true: I want to see like Jesus does. I want Jesus to teach me his ways. I am tired of my own needs, my own limits. I want to be reckless. I want to be like Jesus. And I rejoice that he allows me to follow him on the way. I know the way leads to the cross, but I am done with sitting on the side of the road and hearing him pass by. I want to be with Jesus and am so grateful that he wants me to be with him.

Jesus and Jairus's daughter

The following reflection is by Louis Damani Jones, a fellow at the Gephardt Institute for Civic and Community Engagement and a cohost of the Living Communion *podcast, which can be found anywhere podcasts are located.*

It is as if I'm Peter, walking with Jesus into the home of Jairus. Everyone else is sent away. It is only James, John, and I. I trust Jesus. I love Jesus. Yet, sometimes I think, why me? Why has Jesus trusted me to follow him here into this moment? We step over the threshold into the shadowed stone building. Weeping women can hardly raise their eyes to us as we enter. Jesus asks them why they are weeping. Everyone looks at Jesus with confusion, and some even laugh at him, believing him to be completely out of touch with what is happening. They have not seen what I have seen. They have not seen this man completely transform the ordinary into the kingdom of God, as I have. He told them to leave. The force of his words convicted them in an instant. They were ushered out, and the space changed. Jesus walked to the bed with the father and mother and us alone. That hand that I had seen do so much reached out and touched the lifeless hand of the daughter of Jairus. He wrapped his hand around hers and said, "Talitha cumi." It was as if his life coursed through her as he pulled her from death. Jesus looked at me and asked me to get her something to eat. Jesus is asking me to provide for one he has just lifted from death. Jesus has asked me to participate in the miracle that he has wrought, feeding His sheep.

Jesus on the cross

The following reflection is by the author.

I find myself standing with a small group of Jesus' friends: Mary Magdalene; Salome; Joanna; Mary, mother of James; James and John; and Mary, Jesus' mother. Many others are absent — most notably, Peter. We are standing across the road from where Jesus and the others are crucified, the towering north wall of the city behind us. Here, we might escape the notice of the Romans and the small crowd of important men who have come to mock and gloat; travelers and passersby, too, watch the crucified men, or cast their eyes to the ground. Few notice us here, yet we are close enough to hear the sharp rebukes of the important men, close enough to hear the loud voices of the Romans, close enough to hear the dangerous sound of their metal. Close enough, too, to meet Jesus' eyes.

The other crucified men gasp for air like fish out of water, groaning and cursing. Jesus has been silent, mostly, although he keeps shifting the weight of his body from one side to the other; it reminds me of a child trying to find a comfortable position in bed. I can see that he is gasping for air, too, the way his broken chest rises and falls. He is covered in blood, and great black and purple bruises. I can't imagine his pain, but I am glad it is not me up there.

The absence of so many of his followers makes me wonder what I am doing here. Why watch the end, when I can do nothing to stop it, and nothing to ease his suffering? I wonder whether we are adding to his pain by watching his humiliation.

"We said we would follow him," Mary Magdalene says, not taking her eyes off him. Her jaw is set in that way she has when she is being stubborn. "So, we will follow him to the end."

There is blood on her, too: Her lower lip is swollen and broken where a Roman cuffed her. She had been trying to reach Jesus, hurling insults at his torturers even as her friends restrained her. What would she have done if she had reached him? I don't know, but I admire her spirit. I feel the same rush of anger at the meanness and the violence of the men who stand at the foot of the cross, snapping and biting like dogs. My anger toward them merges with my anger at all the bullies I've ever known — the ones from my childhood, but the ones who seem to own the world, too. The ones who bomb innocent people and steal from the needy, the ones who use their words to scapegoat others.

I suspect that if I had the weapons at hand, I would have no problem using them against those men at the foot of the cross.

I feel angry at God, too — betrayed, maybe. Why does he hold back? Why does he allow the bullies of the world to slaughter and oppress the innocent? I am thinking of the Holocaust, and all the terrorism, and the wars. And I am thinking of Jerusalem, the city behind me, whose inhabitants will be slaughtered en masse by the Romans in just another forty years. Didn't they pray for salvation — if not for themselves, then for their children?

Salome and Joanna and the other Mary are huddled around his mother, as if to make a wall around her. She is watching Jesus, her face drawn and wet with tears. Some of the women are reciting Jewish prayers that I do not recognize, and Mary seems to mouth them silently. A hot, dry wind lifts strands of hair across her face. Although the sky is practically black with storm clouds, it does not smell like rain.

Mary holds her gaze on Jesus.

I follow her eyes to Jesus' face. It is difficult to see those kind eyes struggling against the pain, but I do not look away, and I find him meeting my eyes, too. He sees me — and my anger, and my hurting, and my questions, and his eyes answer me.

Maybe this is why I am here; maybe this is why I stand here, a witness.

On the road to Emmaus

Nelly Sosa is a Catholic communicator, wife, and the mother of three children who never cease to surprise her every day. She blogs for Spanish-speaking Catholics at El Árbol Menta: *www.elarbolmenta. com.*

I am walking to Emmaus with a beloved friend, at night, trying to make sense of these challenging times, and looking for answers. ...

The air is warm, the sky is clear, covered with stars. But it is still dark ...

I hope dawn comes soon.

It has been a rough journey for months. ... I had never prayed so much in my life or entrusted my family and myself to you this much.

Master, you have always protected us; I know this in my heart, but I still have my moments of desolation when I can't find you in the suffering of our brothers and sisters ...

In all those lives lost to the virus ... to violence ... to exploitation of some sort ... to persecution ...

There are days when I can't recognize you in the midst of all the pain around me.

Please listen to the prayers in my heart ... hear my sadness, my confusion, my frustration.

But above all ... let me hear you ... let me see your face. ...

Sustain me when my feet get hurt and my soul becomes weary. Suffering is redemptive. ...

"Was it not necessary that the Messiah should suffer these things and enter into his glory?" you said, and these words resounded deeply into my soul.

In the wait, in the silence, in the loneliness, you are purifying us, O Lord!

I want to cooperate with your plans ... but please, let me feel your loving presence ...

"Stay with us, for it is nearly the evening and the day is almost over."

In the midst of this trial, help me to recognize your voice; bring me your strength so I can totally unite my will to yours, my Good Shepherd.

How to Organize and Run a "Walking with Jesus" Prayer Group

One way to extend your experience of imaginative prayer is to share it with others in a small-group setting. There are many ways to do this:

- Gather a group of trusted friends to start a small prayer group focused on imaginative prayer.
- Start a "Walking with Jesus" prayer group at your parish.
- Introduce imaginative prayer to your older children.
- Introduce imaginative prayer to teens in a youth group or classroom setting.

The following ideas — including session outlines and reading plans — will help you get started. You can get many of these resources as printable downloads from gracewatch.org/imagine.

Gathering a Group

Who can participate in a "Walking with Jesus" prayer group? This book is geared toward older teens and adults who are comfortable with their faith and generally familiar with the Bible. It is written primarily for a Catholic audience, although Christians of any denomination should feel comfortable with the material. (See below for ways to adapt your group session for those who might not fit this target audience.)

If you will be reaching out to others to invite them to your group, you might use the following as a starting point for your message:

> Would you like to get to know Jesus on a deeper, more personal level? What if you could hop in a time machine and walk with Jesus and his friends in first-century Palestine?
>
> With imaginative prayer, you can. Imaginative prayer is a method of meditative prayer popularized by St. Ignatius of Loyola. In imaginative prayer, you let the Holy Spirit guide your imagination as you enter a scene from the Gospels. In imaginative prayer, you don't just read and analyze the Gospel; you live it, directly participating in the story and interacting with the characters. Saint Ignatius encouraged the practice of imaginative prayer as a powerful way to grow in faith in Jesus Christ.
>
> If imaginative prayer sounds interesting to you, join our "Walking with Jesus" prayer group. We'll be using *Imagine You Walked with Jesus: A Guide to Ignatian Contemplative Prayer* to guide our prayer and to help us share our prayer experience with one another. (Include details about the meeting time and sign-up information.)

This message can be placed in your parish bulletin, on flyers, in your parish e-mail newsletter, and on social media.

Ideally, your group will include four to seven people. You want enough people in the group to get several different perspectives on the reading, but if the group gets too large, it could become unwieldy to share one another's stories in any depth. If you have more than seven people, consider splitting into subgroups that meet at the same time.

Before the first meeting, group participants should read the introduction to this book for an overview of the purpose and method of imaginative prayer. Or allow time at the first meeting to present this information to the group in your own words.

Reading Plans

The forty readings provided in this book will keep a small prayer group busy for about nine months, if it meets weekly. Alternatively, your group can plan to meet for a shorter period of time — during a special liturgical season, for example, or to accompany a Bible study focused on a particular Gospel. See the list of reading plans provided on page 225.

Session Outline

A rich experience of imaginative prayer requires time: time to get settled, time to welcome the Holy Spirit, and time to let the imagination "play" in the story.

So, how much time should you allow for your group session? That will depend, in part, on how quiet or talkative your group is, but a good rule of thumb would be to allow sixty to ninety minutes for adults, and forty-five to sixty minutes for youth. See below for ways to adapt this session for quiet groups and for doing imaginative prayer with children.

- **Prepare a prayerful environment for the session.**

Make sure you have comfortable seating, good lighting, tissues, and writing materials for people who want to write their prayer experience (or suggest that people purchase a notebook or journal for this purpose). Ideally, there will be room for participants to spread out (or move to separate areas) during the individual prayer time. Optionally, you can also provide snacks, candles, and (nondistracting) background music to play while people pray.

- **Welcome people as they arrive and give them time to get settled.** If you like, you can use this time to recruit individuals to lead prayer or read the Gospel story.

- **Begin with prayer.** You can use the prayer provided with the Gospel story or supply your own. Allow a period of silence as you welcome the Holy Spirit into your hearts.

- **Read the Gospel story once.** Ask your designated reader to read the story aloud for the group.

- **Discuss the background information and prompt questions.** After reading this information, spend no more than five minutes "setting the scene" as a group. What physical and sensory details might enliven this story? Which characters might offer interesting points of view? Keep the discussion short and focused on a concrete encounter with the Gospel story. You can have a longer conversation about its meaning later.

- **Read the story again.** This time, read it more slowly, savoring each sentence.

- **Invite everyone to reflect on the story individually.** Allow twenty to thirty minutes for this step. Play music or white noise in the background if you find it helpful. After the first few sessions, you may need to adjust the amount of time you spend on this step to fit the personality of your group.

- **Gather again to share your stories.** When the group has gathered again, invite people to share their prayer experience with the group. Those who journaled their experience may want to read what they wrote; others might be more comfortable sharing bits and pieces of their experience. Of course, anyone who is uncomfortable sharing with the group should be allowed to pass. If most or all of your group is uncomfortable sharing their prayer with one another, see the adaptation below.

- **Optionally, discuss the reflection questions.** If you have time and are so inclined, extend your conversation by discussing the questions provided at the end of each chapter.

- **Offer a closing prayer of thanksgiving.** Close the session with a short prayer of thanksgiving. Incorporate the highlights of the group's shared experience and lift up any intentions that may have emerged from the group discussion. For example: "Lord, thanks for inviting us to walk with you in [the setting of the Gospel story] today. Thanks for showing us [whatever insights the group gleaned from its discussion]. We lift up in a special way [any intentions related to the group discussion, such as someone's need for spiritual or physical healing]. We ask all this in your holy name. Amen."

As always, encourage the practice of good group etiquette, ensuring that each person has ample time to speak and that no one dominates the conversation. Affirm the contributions of each person and discourage criticism of anyone's personal prayer experience.

In particular, avoid the temptation to delve into doctrinal or theological discussions of the validity of someone's prayer experience — especially avoid this in the group setting. Such discussions may be interesting and even important, but if they come to dominate the discussion, you are going to end up with a very different type of group. Worse, group members may spend more time "editing" their prayer than letting the Holy Spirit lead them.

However, if someone suggests a scenario that you feel absolutely must be addressed in the group setting (for example, in a youth group), address the issue succinctly, reaffirm the positive aspects of what the person shared, and move on.

Adaptations for "Quiet" Groups

Many people are reluctant to share their personal prayer experiences with others, especially in a group setting. That is not surprising; our spiritual lives touch the very heart of our identity, and imaginative prayer is a deeply personal encounter with Christ. Sharing at that level of vulnerability requires confidence in oneself, as well as trust in others. You might find yourself with a "quiet" group if it includes any of the following:

- young people
- people who did not actively choose the experience (e.g., students in a classroom setting)
- people who are new to the Christian faith
- people who do not feel confident in their prayer life
- people who are naturally shy

If you expect to be introducing imaginative prayer to people who may be uncomfortable with sharing their experience, adapt the session outline above to meet them where they are. Here are some suggestions:

- **Give permission to not share.** Mention up front — in announcements for the group and at the first session — that while sharing is encouraged, no one will be forced to share.
- **Build group trust.** As noted above, trust is key to helping people feel comfortable sharing in a group. For this reason, if you want to introduce imaginative prayer to a group that has gathered for a different purpose (a religious-education program, for example, or a weekend retreat), it may be prudent to schedule the imaginative prayer experience for later in the program. If you have time, you can also have the group do various icebreakers and trust-building exercises before tackling the imaginative prayer experience.
- **Model sharing.** Instead of skipping the sharing step altogether, share your own prayer experience in order to provide a living example of what imaginative prayer might look like, at least for you. If possible, find a collaborator — some brave individual willing to share his experience with the group. (Approach the person ahead of the session — you do not want to put anyone on the spot.) Ideally, your collaborator will have a different approach to imaginative prayer than you do, demonstrating that there is no one "right" way to enter the Gospel in imaginative prayer.
- **Use concrete questions to create opportunities for "safe" sharing.** You might also try leading the group through the prompt questions associated with each Gospel story. Ask group members, for instance, about the sensory details they imagined: What did they see, hear, and smell? What kind of clothes were people wearing? What was the weather like? What facial expressions did they see on different characters at criti-

cal moments in the story? And so on. Asking simple, concrete questions will make it easier for group members to share and will build trust. As the group becomes more comfortable with sharing over the course of several sessions, ask deeper questions (including the reflection questions at the end of each chapter).

- **Omit the discussion of the reflection questions in step 9.** Until group members feel comfortable sharing with one another, skip the reflection questions at the end of each chapter, or replace them with a discussion of the prompt questions as described in the preceding suggestion.

Above all, meet people in your group wherever they happen to be in their spiritual life — just as Jesus did.

Doing Imaginative Prayer with Children

While this book is primarily intended for adults and older teens, you can definitely do imaginative prayer with young people, including children. A full introduction to using imaginative prayer with children would require another book (although see the resources below). However, here are some tips if you want to try it with your own children.

- **Use a kid-friendly Bible translation with older kids.** Both the *Contemporary English Version* and the *Good News Translation* may be easier for middle-grade readers to comprehend. Both are available at the Bible Gateway website. The *Catholic Children's Bible* from Saint Mary's Press uses the *Good News Translation* and includes added features to help children understand key stories:

- **Use a book of Bible stories with younger children.**
  For younger children, use a book of Bible stories;
  the *Catholic Book of Bible Stories* by Laurie Lazzaro
  Knowlton (Zonderkidz) or *The Catholic Bible for Children* by Karine-Marie Amiot, Francois Carmagnac,
  and Christophe Raimbault (Ignatius Press) are both
  good options.
- **Pray alongside older children, then share your experiences.** Introduce older children to imaginative
  prayer by praying alongside them to model the experience. Modify the session outline for group prayer
  (above), shortening the amount of time allowed for
  prayerful meditation to fit the attention span of your
  children. Share your experience with one another —
  you may be surprised at how the Holy Spirit works in
  your children!
- **Try collaborative storytelling with younger children.** With younger children, or older kids not used
  to meditative prayer, try collaborative imaginative
  prayer. Read the Gospel story aloud to your children,
  then draw on the "Imagining the Story" background
  information and prompt questions to help your children imagine themselves in the story. For example: "If
  you could be in this story, who would you like to be —
  Mary or Martha? Or would you be a kid in the room?
  What do you think Jesus looks like in this story? If
  you were there, what would you say?" And so on.

To learn more about teaching children meditative and contemplative prayer, including imaginative prayer, look into the many
resources available from the Catechesis of the Good Shepherd
religious-education program. Also, the Catholic Diocese of Townsville (Australia) regularly teaches meditation and contemplation

to children and youth (see their website, cominghome.org.au, for ideas and resources). And for a more in-depth introduction to using imaginative prayer with children, see Jared Patrick Boyd's *Imaginative Prayer: A Yearlong Guide for Your Child's Spiritual Formation* (IVP Books).

Reading Plans

Readings for Beginners

The following readings are relatively simple, yet rich with possibilities.

- Mary Visits Elizabeth (reading guide #1, Lk 1:39–49)
- The Finding of Jesus in the Temple (reading guide #5, Lk 2:41–51)
- The Miraculous Catch of Fish (reading guide #7, Lk 5:3–11)
- The Wedding at Cana (reading guide #8, Jn 2:1–10)
- Jesus Heals a Paralyzed Man (reading guide #10, Mk 2:1–12)
- Jesus Calms the Stormy Sea (reading guide #12, Mk 4:35–41)
- Jesus Feeds the People (reading guide #18, Mt 14:14–20)
- Jesus Calls Peter to Walk on Water (reading guide #19, Mt 14.22–33)
- Jesus Heals a Blind Man (reading guide #20, Mk 10:46–52)

- Martha and Mary (reading guide #23, Lk 10:38–42)
- Jesus and the Little Children (reading guide #24, Mt 18:1–5; 19:13–15)
- Jesus Invites Himself to Zacchaeus's House (reading guide #25, Lk 19:2–10)
- In the Garden of Gethsemane (reading guide #31, Mt 26:34–46)
- Peter Denies Jesus (reading guide #33, Lk 22:54–62)
- The Crucifixion of Jesus (reading guide #36, Lk 23:33–43)
- On the Road to Emmaus (reading guide #39, Lk 24:13–35)

The Gospel of Matthew
- Following the Star of the Messiah (reading guide #3, Mt 2:1–12)
- The Holy Family Flees to Egypt (reading guide #4, Mt 2:13–15, 19–21)
- Jesus Heals the Centurion's Servant (reading guide #11, Mt 8:5–13)
- Jesus Calls Matthew and Eats with Sinners (reading guide #13, Mt 9:9–13)
- Jesus Feeds the People (reading guide #18, Mt 14:14–20)
- Jesus Calls Peter to Walk on Water (reading guide #19, Mt 14:22–33)
- The Transfiguration of Jesus (reading guide #21, Mt 17:1–8)
- Jesus and the Little Children (reading guide #24, Mt 18:1–5; 19:13–15)
- Jesus Cleanses the Temple (reading guide #28, Mt 21:12–17)
- In the Garden of Gethsemane (reading guide #31, Mt

26:36–46)
- The Resurrection of Jesus (reading guide #38, Mt 28:1–10)

The Gospel of Mark
- John Baptizes Jesus in the Jordan River (reading guide #6, Mk 1:4–11)
- A Busy Day in Capernaum (reading guide #9, Mk 1:29–39)
- Jesus Heals a Paralyzed Man (reading guide #10, Mk 2:1–12)
- Jesus Calms the Stormy Sea (reading guide #12, Mk 4:35–41)
- Jesus Heals a Blind Man (reading guide #20, Mk 10:46–52)
- Jesus Is Betrayed and Arrested (reading guide #32, Mk 14:43–52)
- Jesus before Pilate (reading guide #34, Mk 15:1–20)

The Gospel of Luke
- Mary Visits Elizabeth (reading guide #1, Lk 1:39–49)
- The Birth of Jesus (reading guide #2, Lk 2:1–20)
- The Finding of Jesus in the Temple (reading guide #5, Lk 2:41–51)
- The Miraculous Catch of Fish (reading guide #7, Lk 5:3–11)
- The Daughter of Jairus and the Woman with a Hemorrhage (reading guide #14, Lk 8:40–56)
- Jesus Sends His Disciples to Proclaim the Kingdom (reading guide #15, Lk 10:1–12, 17–20)
- Jesus Heals the Bent Woman (reading guide #16, Lk 13:10–17)
- Martha and Mary (reading guide #23, Lk 10:38–42)

- Jesus Invites Himself to Zacchaeus's House (reading guide #25, Lk 19:2–10)
- Jesus Enters Jerusalem (reading guide #27, Lk 19:35–44)
- The Last Supper (reading guide #30, Lk 22:14–34)
- Peter Denies Jesus (reading guide #33, Lk 22:54–62)
- The Way of the Cross (reading guide #35, Lk 23:26–32)
- The Crucifixion of Jesus (reading guide #36, Lk 23:33–43)
- The Death and Burial of Jesus (reading guide #37, Lk 23:44–56)
- On the Road to Emmaus (reading guide #39, Lk 24:13–35)

The Gospel of John
- The Wedding at Cana (reading guide #8, Jn 2:1–10)
- The Samaritan Woman at the Well (reading guide #17, Jn 4:4–30, 39–42)
- The Woman Caught in Adultery (reading guide #22, Jn 8:2–11)
- The Raising of Lazarus (reading guide #26, Jn 11:1–7, 17–44)
- The Anointing of Jesus (reading guide #29, Jn 12:1–8)
- Jesus Forgives Peter (reading guide #40, Jn 21:1–19)

Advent
Advent is a time of waiting … and preparing to welcome the Lord. In the reading plan below, the first three readings feature themes of anticipation, preparation, and welcome. The fourth reading provides an opportunity to reflect on what it means to imitate Jesus by becoming a little child, just as he did.

- Week 1: Jesus Invites Himself to Zacchaeus's House

(reading guide #25, Lk 19:2–10)
- Week 2: Martha and Mary (reading guide #23, Lk 10:38–42)
- Week 3: Mary Visits Elizabeth (reading guide #1, Lk 1:39–49)
- Week 4: Jesus and the Little Children (reading guide #24, Mt 18:1–5; 19:13–15)

Christmas

Many Christians forget that Christmas is not a single day, but an entire season that ends on the feast of the Baptism of the Lord. Here is a reading plan for the Christmas season:

- Week 1: The Birth of Jesus (reading guide #2, Lk 2:1–20) *or* Following the Star of the Messiah (reading guide #3, Mt 2:1–12)
- Week 2: The Holy Family Flees to Egypt (reading guide #4, Mt 2:13–15, 19–21)
- Week 3: The Finding of Jesus in the Temple (reading guide #5, Lk 2:41–51)
- Week 4: John Baptizes Jesus in the Jordan River (reading guide #6, Mk 1:4–11)

Lent 1

This is the first of two Lenten reading plans; the second, below, suggests praying with readings from the Passion during Holy Week.

- Week 1: The Last Supper (reading guide #30, Lk 22:14–34)
- Week 2: In the Garden of Gethsemane (reading guide #31, Mt 26:36–46) *and/or* Jesus Is Betrayed and Arrested (reading guide #32, Mk 14:43–52) *and/or* Peter Denies Jesus (reading guide #33, Lk 22:54–62)

- Week 3: Jesus before Pilate (reading guide #34, Mk 15:1–20)
- Week 4: The Way of the Cross (reading guide #35, Lk 23:26–32)
- Week 5: The Crucifixion of Jesus (reading guide #36, Lk 23:33–43)
- Week 6: The Death and Burial of Jesus (reading guide #37, Lk 23:44–56)

Lent 2

This second Lenten reading plan is designed to be used during Holy Week.

- Week 1: Jesus Feeds the People (reading guide #18, Mt 14:14–20)
- Week 2: Jesus Calls Peter to Walk on Water (reading guide #19, Mt 14:22–33)
- Week 3: Jesus Heals a Blind Man (reading guide #20, Mk 10:46–52)
- Week 4: The Woman Caught in Adultery (reading guide #22, Jn 8:2–11)
- Week 5: The Raising of Lazarus (reading guide #26, Jn 11:1–7, 17–44)
- Week 6: Jesus Cleanses the Temple (reading guide #28, Mt 21:12–17)
- Week 7: The Anointing of Jesus (reading guide #29, Jn 12:1–8)

Holy Week

This reading plan can be used by itself during Holy Week, or in addition to the Lent 2 reading plan above.

- Palm Sunday: Jesus Enters Jerusalem (reading guide

#27, Lk 19:35–44)

- Monday: The Last Supper (reading guide #30, Lk 22:14–34)
- Tuesday: In the Garden of Gethsemane (reading guide #31, Mt 26:36–46)
- Wednesday: Jesus Is Betrayed and Arrested (reading guide #32, Mk 14:43–52)
- Thursday: Peter Denies Jesus (reading guide #33, Lk 22:54–62) *and/or* Jesus before Pilate (reading guide #34, Mk 15:1–20)
- Friday: The Way of the Cross (reading guide #35, Lk 23:26–32) *and/or* The Crucifixion of Jesus (reading guide #36, Lk 23:33–43)
- Saturday: The Death and Burial of Jesus (reading guide #37, Luke 23:44–56)

Easter

The Easter season lasts seven weeks, from Easter Sunday through Pentecost. The first three weeks of this plan feature stories of the Resurrection; the remaining four weeks focus on themes of healing, renewal, and the call to discipleship.

- Week 1: The Resurrection of Jesus (reading guide #38, Mt 28:1–10)
- Week 2: On the Road to Emmaus (reading guide #39, Lk 24:13–35)
- Week 3: Jesus Forgives Peter (reading guide #40, Jn 21:1–19)
- Week 4: The Daughter of Jairus and the Woman with a Hemorrhage (reading guide #14, Lk 8:40–56)
- Week 5: Jesus Calls Matthew and Eats with Sinners (reading guide #13, Mt 9:9–13)
- Week 6: The Wedding at Cana (reading guide #8, Jn

2:1–10)
- Week 7: Jesus Sends His Disciples to Proclaim the Kingdom (reading guide #15, Lk 10:1–12, 17–20)

Mysteries of the Rosary

If you pray the Rosary alone or with a group, this reading plan will enrich your meditation on the mysteries of the Rosary. Note that several mysteries do not have corresponding reading guides in this book, although you can download them from gracewatch.org/imagine, or simply read the Scripture texts on your own, using the method provided here as a guide. Also, the last two Glorious Mysteries do not have corresponding Gospel readings, and therefore references are omitted.

The Joyful Mysteries
1. The Annunciation (Lk 1:26–38)
2. The Visitation of Mary (reading guide #1, Lk 1:39–49)
3. The Birth of Jesus (reading guide #2, Lk 2:1–20)
4. The Presentation in the Temple (Lk 2:22–38)
5. The Finding of Jesus in the Temple (reading guide #5, Lk 2:41–51)

The Luminous Mysteries (or Mysteries of Light)
1. John Baptizes Jesus in the Jordan River (reading guide #6, Mk 1:4–11)
2. The Wedding at Cana (reading guide #8, Jn 2:1–10)
3. The Proclamation of the Kingdom (reading guide #15, Lk 10:1–12, 17–20)
4. The Transfiguration of Jesus (reading guide #21, Mt 17:1–8)
5. The Last Supper (reading guide #30, Lk 22:14–34)

The Sorrowful Mysteries

1. The Agony in the Garden of Gethsemane (reading guide #31, Mt 26:36–46)
2. The Scourging at the Pillar (reading guide #34, Mk 15:1–20)
3. The Crowning with Thorns (reading guide #34, Mk 15:1–20)
4. The Way of the Cross (reading guide #35, Lk 23:26–32)
5. The Crucifixion of Jesus (reading guide #36, Lk 23:33–43 *and* reading guide #37, Lk 23:44–56)

The Glorious Mysteries

1. The Resurrection of Jesus (reading guide #38, Mt 28:1–10 *and/or* reading guide #39, Lk 24:13–35 *and/or* reading guide #40, Jn 21:1–19)
2. The Ascension (Acts 1:6–12)
3. The Descent of the Holy Spirit (Acts 2:1–13)
4. The Assumption of Mary
5. The Coronation of Mary

Thirty More Readings for Imaginative Prayer

If you or members of your prayer group are looking for more readings for imaginative prayer, here are some suggestions. Many (but not all) of these additional readings are recommended by Saint Ignatius in his *Spiritual Exercises*.

You can download reflection guides for some of these readings from gracewatch.org/imagine.

- The Annunciation (Lk 1:26–38)
- The Circumcision (Lk 2:21)
- The Presentation (Lk 2:22–38)
- The Hidden Life of Jesus (Lk 2:51–52)
- The Temptation of Christ (Lk 4:1–13; Mt 4:1–11)

- Jesus Calls His First Disciples (Jn 1:35–51)
- Jesus Heals on the Sabbath (Mk 3:1–6)
- Jesus Cures a Demoniac (Mk 5:1–20)
- Jesus Cures the Paralytic at Bethzatha (Jn 5:1–18)
- Jesus Cures the Canaanite Woman's Daughter (Mk 7:24–30)
- Jesus Cures the Deaf and Mute Man (Mk 7:31–37)
- "I Am the Bread of Life" (Jn 6:22–69)
- Peter Confesses Jesus Is the Messiah (Mt 16:13–23)
- Jesus Cures Ten Lepers (Lk 17:11–19)
- Jesus Raises a Young Man from the Dead (Lk 7:11–17)
- Jesus Cures a Man Born Blind (Jn 9:1–12)
- Jesus Forgives the Sinful Woman (Lk 7:36–50)
- The Widow's Mite (Mk 12:41–44)
- Jesus Washes the Disciples' Feet (Jn 13:1–20)
- The Agony in the Garden and the Arrest of Jesus (Mk 14:32–52; Lk 22:39–53)
- The Trial before Pilate (Jn 18:28–19:16)
- The Crucifixion and Death of Jesus (Jn 19:16–37)
- The Resurrected Jesus Appears to His Mother*
- The Resurrected Jesus Appears to Three Women (Mk 16:1–11)
- The Resurrected Jesus Appears to Peter (Lk 24:33–34)
- The Resurrected Jesus Appears to the Disciples in the Upper Room (Jn 20:19–23)
- The Resurrected Jesus Appears to Thomas (Jn 20:24–29)
- The Great Commission (Mt 28:16–20)
- The Ascension (Acts 1:6–12)
- The Resurrected Jesus Appears to Paul (Acts 9:1–19)

*There is no Gospel account of the resurrected Jesus appearing to Mary, but Saint Ignatius finds it a fitting subject for meditation.

Acknowledgments

I would like to acknowledge and thank the many people who helped me produce this book.

Rachelle Linner critiqued the first draft of this book in light of her experience with spiritual direction and the Jewish context of the New Testament; her wisdom and advice were especially helpful in improving the prompts and the reflection questions. Several of the reflection questions were suggested by her, and I am grateful for her contributions.

Betty Singer-Towns brought a sharp eye and pastoral sensitivity to her thorough review of the first draft, suggesting several new reflection questions that were retained in the final manuscript.

Brian Singer-Towns brought his extensive experience editing Bibles for Saint Mary's Press to his review of the manuscript and made several key suggestions for improving the introduction and the prayer process. Barbara Allaire, Jim Allaire, and Pat Daoust offered encouraging feedback (as always!). Finally, Allison Gingras critiqued the small-group dimension of the book from the perspective of someone with many years of experience leading small prayer and study groups.

Sr. Julia Walsh, FSPA, Rachelle Linner, Louis Damani Jones, and Nelly Sosa wrote examples of imaginative prayer-journal entries. Sr. Walsh blogs and podcasts at MessyJesusBusiness.com. Ms. Linner is a freelance writer, reviewer, and spiritual director who is a frequent contributor to *Give Us This Day*. Mr. Jones is a fellow at the Gephardt Institute for Civic and Community Engagement and a cohost of the *Living Communion* podcast. Ms. Sosa blogs for Spanish-speaking Catholics at *El Árbol Menta*: www. elarbolmenta.com.

I would also like to thank Mary Beth Giltner, senior acquisitions editor at Our Sunday Visitor, and the entire OSV team for their work on this project.

Last but not least, I would like to thank my family for their ongoing support and encouragement, especially my parents, Norman and Pat Daoust, who were the first to teach me the Faith; and my wife, Susan Windley-Daoust, who offered her theological expertise as well as invaluable support and encouragement.

Bibliography

Alphin, George. "A New Testament Geography: Description, Perspectives, and Implications for the Field of Geography." PhD diss., Louisiana State University, 2001. digitalcommons.lsu.edu/gradschool_disstheses/261.

Brown, Raymond E., Joseph A. Fitzmyer, and Roland E. Murphy, eds. *The New Jerome Biblical Commentary*, New Jersey: Prentice-Hall, 1990.

"Capernaum." In *The Oxford Companion to the Bible*, edited by Bruce M. Metzger, Michael D. Coogan, and Sherman Elbridge Johnson. Oxford Biblical Studies Online. Accessed February 4, 2021. http://www.oxfordbiblicalstudies.com /article/opr/t120/e0128.

Cohney, Shelley. "The Jewish Temples: The Second Temple." Jewish Virtual Library. https://www.jewishvirtuallibrary.org /the-second-temple.

Confraternity of Christian Doctrine, Inc. *New American Bible*, revised edition. Last modified March 9, 2011. https://bible .usccb.org/bible.

Curtis, Adrian. "Jerusalem in New Testament Times." In *Oxford*

Bible Atlas. Oxford Biblical Studies Online. Accessed February 4, 2021. http://www.oxfordbiblicalstudies.com /article/book/obso-9780191001581/obso-9780191001581 -chapter-22.

Dark, Ken. "Has Jesus' Nazareth House Been Found?" *Biblical Archaeology Review* 41 no. 2 (March/April 2015). www .baslibrary.org/biblical-archaeology-review/41/2/7.

"Death & Bereavement in Judaism: Ancient Burial Practices." Jewish Virtual Library. https://www.jewishvirtuallibrary.org /ancient-burial-practices.

"Family." In *The Oxford Companion to the Bible*, edited by Bruce M. Metzger, Michael D. Coogan, and David F. Wright. Oxford Biblical Studies Online. Accessed February 4, 2021. http://www.oxfordbiblicalstudies.com/article/opr/t120 /e0253.

Feinberg Vamosh, Miriam. "What People in Ancient Israel Really Wore." Haaretz, December 26, 2013. www.haaretz.com /archaeology/.premium-what-people-in-ancient-israel -really-wore-1.5304235.

"Galilee." In *A Dictionary of the Bible*, edited by W. R. F. Browning. Oxford Biblical Studies Online. Accessed February 4, 2021. http://www.oxfordbiblicalstudies.com/article/opr/t94 /e718.

Gallagher, Timothy M. *Meditation and Contemplation: An Ignatian Guide to Praying with Scripture.* New York: Crossroad Publishing Company, 2008.

Geggel, Laura. "Jesus Wasn't the Only Man to Be Crucified. Here's the History behind This Brutal Practice." LiveScience, April 19, 2019. https://www.livescience.com/65283 -crucifixion-history.html.

Hahn, Scott. "The Hunt for the Fourth Cup." Catholic Answers, September 1, 1991. https://www.catholic.com/magazine /print-edition/hunt-for-the-fourth-cup.

Hedges, Chris. "Scholars Debate Jesus' Route to Crucifixion." *South Florida Sun-Sentinel*, February 3, 1990. https://www .sun-sentinel.com/news/fl-xpm-1990-02-03-9001220637 -story.html.

Henriksen Garroway, Kristine. "The World of Children in the Hebrew Bible." The Bible and Interpretation, November 2018. https://bibleinterp.arizona.edu/articles/world -children-hebrew-bible.

"The House of Peter: The Home of Jesus in Capernaum?" *Bible History Daily*. Biblical Archaeology Society, January 27, 2021. https://www.biblicalarchaeology.org/daily /biblical-sites-places/biblical-archaeology-sites/the -house-of-peter-the-home-of-jesus-in-capernaum/.

"Houses, Furniture, Utensils." In *The Oxford Companion to the Bible*, edited by Bruce M. Metzger, Michael D. Coogan, and Kenneth E. Bailey. Oxford Biblical Studies Online. Accessed February 3, 2021. http://www.oxfordbiblicalstudies .com/article/opr/t120/e0335.

"The Jewish Temples: Jerusalem during the Second Temple Period (516 BCE–70 CE)." Jewish Virtual Library. Accessed February 3, 2021. https://www.jewishvirtuallibrary.org/jerusalem- during-the-second-temple-period.

"Judah." In *The Oxford Encyclopedia of Archaeology in the Near East*, edited by Eric M. Meyers and Avi Ofer. Oxford Biblical Studies Online. Accessed February 4, 2021. http:// www.oxfordbiblicalstudies.com/article/opr/t256/e568.

Korb, Scott. *Life in Year One: What the World Was Like in First-Century Palestine*. New York: Penguin Publishing Group, 2010.

Loarte, J. A. "Life of Mary (VI): Visitation to Saint Elizabeth." Opus Dei, March 17, 2014. https://opusdei.org/en-us/article/life -of-mary-vi-visitation-to-saint-elizabeth/.

Laughlin, John C. H. "Capernaum: From Jesus' Time and After." *Bib-*

lical Archaeology Review 19, no. 5 (September/October 1993). https://www.baslibrary.org/biblical-archaeology-review /19/5/10.

Levine, Amy-Jill, and Marc Zvi Brettler, eds. *The Jewish Annotated New Testament: New Revised Standard Version Bible Translation.* Oxford, Uk: Oxford University Press, 2017. Kindle.

Lohfink, Gerhard. *Jesus of Nazareth: What He Wanted, Who He Was.* Collegevill, MN: Liturgical Press, 2012.

"Lord's Supper." In *The Oxford Companion to the Bible*, edited by Bruce M. Metzger, Michael D. Coogan, and I. Howard Marshall. Oxford Biblical Studies Online. Accessed February 4, 2021. http://www.oxfordbiblicalstudies.com /article/opr/t120/e0442.

Martin, James. *The Jesuit Guide to (Almost) Everything: A Spirituality for Real Life.* New York: HarperOne, 2010.

Matassa, Lidia D. *Invention of the First-Century Synagogue.* Edited by Jason M. Silverman and J. Murray Watson. Atlanta: SBL Press, 2018. https://www.sbl-site.org/assets/pdfs /pubs/9780884143208_OA.pdf.

"Nazareth." In *The Oxford Companion to the Bible*, edited by Bruce M. Metzger, Michael D. Coogan, and Edwin D. Freed. Oxford Biblical Studies Online. Accessed February 4, 2021. http://www.oxfordbiblicalstudies.com/article/opr/t120 /e0520.

"Palestine." In *A Dictionary of the Bible*, edited by W. R. F. Browning. Oxford Biblical Studies Online. Accessed February 4, 2021. http://www.oxfordbiblicalstudies.com/article/opr/t94 /e1399.

Patrich, Joseph. "Reconstructing the Magnificent Temple Herod Built." *Bible Review* 4, no. 5 (October 1988). https://www .baslibrary.org/bible-review/4/5/3.

Pope, Msgr. Charles. "What Were Typical Homes Like in Jesus'

Time?" Communion in Mission, July 1, 2014. http://blog.adw.org/2014/07/what-were-typical-homes-like-in-jesus-time/.

———. "What Sort of Clothing Did People in Jesus' Time Wear?" Communion in Mission, March 29, 2017. http://blog.adw.org/2017/03/sort-clothing-people-jesus-time-wear/.

———. "What Were Weddings Like in Jesus' Day?" *Catholic Standard*, August 1, 2019. https://cathstan.org/posts/what-were-weddings-like-in-jesus-day-2.

Puhl, Louis J. *The Spiritual Exercises of St. Ignatius: A New Translation Based on Studies in the Language of the Autograph*. United States: Newman Press, 1951.

Religion News Service. "A Long, Cold Road to Bethlehem." *Los Angeles Times*, December 23, 1995. https://www.latimes.com/archives/la-xpm-1995-12-23-me-17102-story.html.

Ritmeyer, Kathleen. "Reconstructing Herod's Temple Mount in Jerusalem." *Biblical Archaeology Review* 15, no. 6 (November/December 1989). https://www.baslibrary.org/biblical-archaeology-review/15/6/1.

Saint Mary's Press. "The Life and Times of First-Century Palestine." 2010. www.smp.org/resourcecenter/resource/4011/.

"Samaria." In *The Oxford Companion to the Bible*, edited by Bruce M. Metzger, Michael D. Coogan, and Mary Joan Winn Leith. Oxford Biblical Studies Online. Accessed February 4, 2021. http://www.oxfordbiblicalstudies.com/article/opr/t120/e0646.

Smith, Daniel. "The Setting of the Last Supper: A Triclinium." Redeemer of Israel, March 24, 2016. http://www.redeemerofisrael.org/2012/04/setting-of-last-supper-triclinium.html.

Standaert, Nicolas. "The Composition of Place: Creating Space for an Encounter." *Way* 46, no. 1 (January 2007): 7–20. www.theway.org.uk/back/461Standaert.pdf.

Wallace, Daniel B. "Passover in the Time of Jesus." Bible.org, May 28, 2004. https://bible.org/article/passover-time-jesus.

"Weddings." In *The Oxford Companion to the Bible*, edited by Bruce M. Metzger, Michael D. Coogan, and Gordon J. Wenham. Oxford Biblical Studies Online. Accessed February 4, 2021. http://www.oxfordbiblicalstudies.com /article/opr/t120/e0764.

"Weddings in the Bible." Women in the Bible. Accessed February 6, 2021. https://www.womeninthebible.net/bible-extras /weddings-in-the-bible/.

Windle, Bryan. "Did First-Century Nazareth Exist?" *Bible Archaeology Report*, August 9, 2018. biblearchaeologyreport .com/2018/08/09/did-first-century-nazareth-exist/.

Worrall, Simon. "The Little Town of Bethlehem Has a Surprising History." *National Geographic*, December 23, 2017. https://www.nationalgeographic.com/news/2017/12 /bethlehem-christ-birth-blincoe.

About the Author

Everyone looks up to Jerry Windley-Daoust, and not just because he is two meters tall (that's just about 6' 7" for those still resisting the metric system): He is also the author of more than two dozen books on topics such as Catholic social teaching, family spirituality, and Ignatian prayer. Even more impressively, he spent ten years as a stay-at-home dad for his five children while his wife taught theology at Saint Mary's University of Minnesota. He took an MA in pastoral ministry from the same institution, despite submitting a 250-page master's thesis that his adviser never finished reading. Lately, Jerry has also been writing essays, poetry, novels, and award-winning short stories grounded in Christian hope. You can find him hiking along the Mississippi River with his family on many Sunday afternoons; however, an easier way to track him down would be to find his portfolio website, Windhovering.com, which takes its name from "The Windhover," a poem by one of his favorite poets, G. M. Hopkins.

YOU MIGHT ALSO LIKE

What Do You Really Want? St. Ignatius Loyola and the Art of Discernment *Jim Manney*

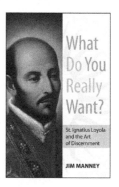

We can find answers through learning the art of discernment- the wisdom that enables us to see and interpret the leading of the Holy Spirit as it is manifested in the inner lives of our hearts. The great master of this art was St. Ignatius Loyola, author of The Spiritual Exercises, who believed that the ability to discern the spirits is one of the most important skills a Christian could have. Ignatius believed that the answer to the question "What Should I Do?" is found in the shifting sea of feelings, insights, leadings, and intuitions of our affective lives.

What Do You Really Want? shows us how to understand these emotions and use what we learn to make the choices that best serve God and bring his love to the people in our lives. It shows the truth of one of Ignatius's greatest insights-that when we find what we really want, we find what God wants too, because the deepest desires of our hearts were placed there by God.

YOU MIGHT ALSO LIKE

Prayer: The Breath of New Life
Pope Francis

What is prayer and why is it so important? Pope Francis teaches that prayer is the "heartbeat of the Church" and our "yes" to an encounter with God:

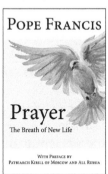

In the human body, there are some essential functions, such as breathing and the beating of the heart.

I like to imagine that the personal and communal prayer of us Christians is the breath, the heartbeat of the Church, which instills its strength in the service of those who work, study, teach; which makes fruitful the knowledge of educated people and the humility of simple people; which gives hope to the tenacity of those who fight injustice.

Prayer is our saying "yes" to the Lord, to His love that reaches us; it is welcoming the Holy Spirit who, without ever growing weary, pours out love and life upon all.

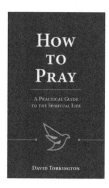